Reprint Publishing

FÜR MENSCHEN, DIE AUF ORIGINALE STEHEN.

www.reprintpublishing.com

Hans Christian Andersen.

Heath's Modern Language Series.

Bilderbuch ohne Bilder

von

Hans Christian Andersen.

Illustrated School Edition.

WITH ENGLISH NOTES AND A GERMAN-ENGLISH VOCABULARY

BY

Dr. Wilhelm Bernhardt.

BOSTON, U. S. A.

D. C. HEATH & CO., PUBLISHERS.

1899.

Printed by Carl H. Heintzemann, Boston, Mass.

PREFACE.

Hans Christian Andersen was born at Odensee, on the island of Fünen, April 2nd, 1805, and died at Copenhagen, August 6th, 1875. Soon after the death of his father, who was a poor shoemaker, the boy went to Copenhagen, to obtain a higher education. After many adversities and hardships he finally found generous friends who helped him in his distress, and application having been made by one of them to the king of Denmark, he was placed at an advanced school at public expense.

Already, in his early youth, Andersen displayed a talent for poetry, and more especially for story-telling. At the close of his university studies, in 1830, having obtained pecuniary aid from the king, he traveled through England, Sweden, Germany, Switzerland, France and Italy; his charming "*Sketches of Travel*" being the fruit of these extended tours. In 1834 he produced a successful romance, entitled "*The Improvisatore*," in which the scenery and manners of Italy are depicted in a glowing style and with admirable fidelity. Another novel, called "*Only a Fiddler*," which appeared

in 1838, presents some striking pictures from the poet's own
early life.   His original genius, however, became most con-
spicuous in his *"Fairy Tales,"* which are characterized by
quaint humor, rich imagination and sometimes by deep
pathos.   Among his minor writings few are better known or
more admired than his *"Picture-Book without Pictures"*
(1841), which contains a series of the finest imaginative
sketches.

In his autobiography Andersen says : " My little book,
'Picture-Book without Pictures' appears, to judge from the
reviews and the number of editions, to have obtained an
extraordinary popularity in Germany.   One of those who
first announced it, added : *'Many of these pictures offer ma-
terial for narratives and novels—yes, one gifted with fancy
might create romances out of them.'*   A couple of translations
appeared in England, and the English critics gave the
little book very high praise, calling it 'an Iliad in a nut-
shell.' —"

In America, too, Andersen's " Picture-Book without Pictures" has made many warm friends, and even enthusiastic
admirers.   For years this little book has been in use in some
of my German classes, where I have had ample opportunity
to watch the favorable impression which these charming
sketches made upon the minds of my students, and it was
the result of my observations in the class-room which induced
me to prepare this School Edition.   I found that the "Pic-

ture-Book without Pictures" is admirably adapted to teach beginners the language and at the same time to awaken their interest for scientific questions, as the stories abound in allusions to facts from the wide fields of Geography, Ethnology, Archæology and History, more especially the history of literature and the arts. Being offered such a charming field for translation, the students were imbued from the very beginning with an interest in the little stories which did not flag at any portion of the book. This observation alone was sufficient to recommend the "Picture-Book" to me as a most valuable acquisition. The "Notes," therefore, while by no means failing to assist the student in surmounting the linguistic difficulties, are especially intended to explain all allusions to scientific questions, of whatever nature they may be. Besides this, the grammatical notes are made complete in themselves without reference to any grammar, so that the student, supported by the complete "German-English Vocabulary" which has been added, does not need any further help for the study and enjoyment of the book.

The fact that in this "School" Edition I have omitted three of the stories of the original text, will, as I confidently hope, not only be excused, but commended by all teachers who like myself have used the former edition.

Finally, the attention of those teachers who desire to make their lessons as attractive and profitable to the students as possible, is called to the excellent opportunity which i⸴

offered them for preparing a Picture-Album, illustrating many scenes of our text.*

It only remains to acknowledge my indebtedness to my friend Professor J. H. DILLARD, of Tulane University of Louisiana, New Orleans, who while faithfully reading proof with me, has frequently suggested changes which were always improvements.

WILHELM BERNHARDT.

WASHINGTON HIGH SCHOOL.
Washington, D. C., October 1st, 1891.

*At a merely nominal expense I have procured for my classes from the Soule Photograph Co., Boston, the following photographs which bear reference to the Picture-Book, and which are given here by their numbers in the Catalogue published by the company named above: —

Nos. 2255 — 2263 — 2595 — 2947 — 3498 — 3500 — 3509 — 4687 — 4754 — 4806 — 5112 — 5145 — 5152 — 5165 — 5168 — 5223 — 5229 — 5231 — 5244 — 5254 — 5271 — 5326 — 5421 — 6162 — 6263 — 8639 — 8668. Send fifteen cents for a copy of their catalogue, which gives sizes and prices.

Es ist sonderbar! Wenn ich am[1] allerwärmsten und innig=
sten empfinde[2], so ist[3] mir, als wären[4] mir[5] Hände und
Zunge gebunden; ich kann nicht recht wiedergeben, nicht recht
aussprechen, was in mir vorgeht; und doch bin ich ein Maler,
das sagt mir mein Auge, das sagen alle, die meine Skizzen und [5]
Blätter sahen.

Ich bin ein armer Bursche, ich wohne in einem der engsten
Gäßchen[6], aber an Licht gebricht[7] es mir nicht, denn ich wohne
hoch oben und habe eine Aussicht auf die Dächer. Während
der ersten Tage, nachdem ich in die Stadt gezogen[8], war es [10]
mir[9] gar enge und einsam; statt des Waldes und der grünen
Hügel erhoben sich nur schwarze Schornsteine an meinem Hori=
zonte. Nicht e i n e n[10] Freund besaß ich, nicht e i n bekanntes
Gesicht begrüßte mich.

Eines Abends[11] stand ich ganz betrübt am Fenster; ich öff= [15]
nete es und blickte hinaus[12]. Ach! Welche Freude erfüllte
mein Herz! Ich sah ein bekanntes Gesicht, ein rundes, freund=
liches Antlitz, das meines besten Freundes aus der Heimat:
das Antlitz des Mondes. Der liebe, alte Mond war unver=
ändert ganz genau derselbe, wie er[13] einst durch die Weiden= [20]
bäume am Moore zu mir herniederblickte. Ich warf ihm Kuß=
hände zu[14], und er schien weit in mein Kämmerchen herein[15]

und versprach, daß er jeden Abend, wenn er ausginge, einige
Augenblicke zu mir hereinschauen wolle[16]. Dieses Versprechen
hat er auch redlich gehalten. Schade[17], daß er nur so kurze
Zeit verweilen kann. Jedesmal, wenn er kommt, erzählt er
dies oder jenes, was er die vorige Nacht[18] oder denselben Abend
gesehen hat. „Male du nur[19] das, was ich erzähle,“ sagte er
bei seinem ersten Besuche, „und du wirst ein recht hübsches Bil=
derbuch erhalten.“ Das habe ich nun viele Abende gethan.
Ich könnte nach meiner Art ein neues „Tausend und eine
Nacht“[20] in Bildern bringen, aber die Zahl würde doch wohl[21]
zu groß sein. Die[22], welche ich hier gebe, sind nicht außer der
Reihe gewählt, sondern folgen, wie ich sie gehört habe. Ein
großer genialer Maler, ein Dichter oder Tonkünstler kann etwas
mehr daraus machen, wenn er Lust hat; was ich zeichne, sind
nur flüchtige Umrisse auf dem Papiere, dazwischen meine eige=
nen Gedanken, denn nicht jeden Abend kam der Mond; oft
trennte uns eine Wolke oder zwei.

Erster Abend.

„In der vergangenen Nacht,“ das sind des Mondes eigene
Worte, „glitt ich durch die klare Luft Indien's; ich spiegelte
mich in dem Ganges[1] und meine Strahlen machten den Ver=
such, durch das dichte Geflechte der[2] wie eine Schildkrötenschale

gewölbten Platanen zu bringen.   Da hüpfte aus dem Dickicht
ein Hindu=Mädchen ³, leicht wie eine Gazelle, schön wie Eva ⁴.
Es war eine so luftige und doch so anmutig und scharf ausge=
prägte Erscheinung, diese Tochter Indien's : ich konnte durch
die zarte Haut den Gedanken sehen.   Die dornigen Lianen ⁵
zerrissen ihre Sandalen, aber schnell schritt sie vorwärts ⁶; das
Wild, vom Flusse kommend, wo es seinen Durst gestillt hatte,
sprang scheu vorüber ⁷, denn das Mädchen hielt in der ⁸ Hand
eine brennende Lampe ; ich konnte das frische Blut in den feinen
Fingern gewahren, die sie zu einem Schirm über der Flamme
wölbte.   Sie näherte sich dem Flusse, setzte die Lampe auf den
Strom und sie ⁹ glitt dahin ¹⁰; die Flamme flackerte, als wollte ¹¹
sie erlöschen ; aber sie blieb doch brennen und des Mädchens
schwarze, funkelnde Augen hinter der ¹² Augenlider langen Sei=
benfransen folgten ihr mit seelenvollem Blick.   Sie wußte, daß,
wenn die Lampe fortbrannte, so weit sie dieser mit den Augen
folgen konnte, ihr Geliebter noch lebte ; erlosch ¹³ sie aber früher,
so war er tot.   Und die Lampe brannte und flammte; sie sank
auf die ¹⁴ Knie und betete.   Neben ihr im Grase lag eine glatte
Schlange, sie aber dachte nur an ¹⁵ Brama ¹⁶ und ihren Bräu=
tigam.   „„Er lebt,"" jubelte sie; „„er lebt!"" hallte es von
den Bergen wieder ¹⁷, „„er lebt!""

Zweiter Abend.

„Gestern," so erzählte mir der Mond, „blickte ich in einen engen, von[1] Häusern rings umschlossenen Hof hinunter[2]. Da lag eine Gluckhenne mit elf Küchlein; ein niebliches kleines Mädchen sprang um sie herum[3]; die Henne gluckte und breitete erschrocken ihre Flügel über die Kleinen aus[4]. Da kam der Vater des Mädchens; er schalt, und ich glitt weiter, ohne ferner daran[5] zu denken. Heute Abend aber, es ist nur wenige Minuten her[6], blickte ich wieder in denselben Hof hinein[7].

Da war alles still; bald aber kam das kleine Mädchen, schlich sich ganz leise bis an das Hühnerhaus, schob den Riegel zurück[8] und schlüpfte zu der Henne und den Küchlein hinein[9]; diese schrieen laut auf[10] und flatterten herum[11]; die Kleine lief hinterher[12]: das sah ich deutlich, denn ich blickte durch ein Loch in der Mauer. Ich zürnte dem bösen Kinde, und freute mich, als der[13] Vater kam und noch heftiger als gestern schalt und sie am Arme faßte; sie bog den Kopf zurück[14], die blauen Augen waren mit großen Thränen gefüllt. „„Was machst du hier?"" fragte er. Sie weinte. „„Ich wollte die Henne küssen und sie wegen gestern um[15] Verzeihung bitten, aber das wagte ich nicht, dir zu sagen!""

Und der Vater küßte die holde Unschuld auf die Stirn, ich aber küßte ihr[16] die Augen und den Mund."

Dritter Abend.

„Ich habe heute[1] Abend einer deutschen Komödie beige=
wohnt,“ erzählte der Mond. „Es war in einem kleinen Städt=
chen. Ein Stall war in ein Theater verwandelt, das heißt:
die Stände waren geblieben und zu[2] Logen[3] ausgeputzt; das
ganze Holzwerk war mit buntem Papier überzogen; unter der 5
niedrigen Decke hing ein kleiner eiserner Kronleuchter, und da=
mit er wie in den großen Theatern verschwinden konnte, wenn
das „„Klingling““ der Glocke des Souffleurs[4] erschallte, war
über ihm eine umgekehrte große Tonne angebracht.

„„Klingling!““ und der kleine eiserne Kronleuchter machte 10
einen Satz von einer halben Elle und verschwand in die[5] Tonne;
und nun wußte man, daß die Komödie anfing. Ein junger
Fürst mit seiner Gemahlin, die eben durch das Städtchen
reisten, wohnten der Vorstellung bei[6]; darum war das Haus
gedrängt voll. Nur unter dem Kronleuchter war es wie ein 15
kleiner Krater; dort saß keine Menschenseele, denn die Lichter
tropften: „„Tropf! Tropf!““ Ich sah alles, denn es war
brinnen so warm, daß man alle Luken geöffnet hatte. Draußen
standen die Knechte und Mägde und guckten durch die Luken,
obgleich die Polizei mit[7] drinnen saß und mit dem Stocke drohte. 20
Dicht am Orchester erblickte man das junge Fürstenpaar in
zwei alten Lehnsesseln, in denen sonst der Bürgermeister und
die Frau Bürgermeisterin Platz nahmen; heute mußten diese
aber auf hölzernen Bänken sitzen, gleich den anderen gewöhn=

lichen Bürgersleuten. „„Jetzt sieht man, daß höher[8] über
hoch geht!"" bemerkten im stillen die Damen; das Ganze
erhielt dadurch einen noch festlichern Anstrich; der Kronleuchter
machte Sätze, dem Pöbel[9] wurden die Finger geklopft, und ich,
der Mond — wohnte der Vorstellung bis zum Schluß bei[10]."

Vierter Abend.

„Gestern," fing der Mond an[1], „blickte ich auf das bewegte
Paris nieder[2]; mein Auge drang in die Gemächer des Louvre[3].
Eine alte Großmutter, ärmlich gekleidet, — sie gehörte den ge-
ringeren Klassen an[4], — folgte einem der untergeordneten Bedienten in den großen, leeren Thronsaal; dieser war es, den sie
sehen wollte, sehen mußte; es hatte ihr manches kleine Opfer,
viele Worte gekostet, ehe sie so weit gelangte. Sie faltete ihre
mageren Hände und blickte andächtig umher[5], als befände[6] sie
sich in einem Gotteshause. „„Hier war es!"" sagte sie,
„„hier!"" und sie näherte sich dem Throne, von dem der
reiche[7], mit goldenen Franſen beſetzte Samt herabhing.
„„Da!"" rief sie, „„da!"" und sie kniete und küßte den
Purpurteppich — ich glaube, sie weinte. „„Dieser Samt
war es aber nicht,"" sagte der Bediente, und ein Lächeln spielte
um seinen Mund. „„Aber hier war es doch,"" erwiderte die
Frau; „„so sah es doch aus[8]."" — „„So und doch nicht

so,"" antwortete er; „„die Fenster waren eingeschlagen, die Thüren ausgehoben, auf dem Fußboden floß Blut! — S i e* kann doch sagen: Mein Enkel ist[10] auf dem Throne Frank= reichs gestorben."" — „„Gestorben!"" wiederholte die alte Frau. — Ich glaube nicht, daß weiter etwas gesprochen wurde; 5 auch verließen sie bald den Saal. Die Abenddämmerung ver= schwand, und mein Licht bestrahlte doppelt hell den reichen Samt auf dem Throne Frankreichs. Für[11] wen hältst du wohl die alte Frau? — Ich werde dir eine Geschichte erzählen: Es geschah in der Julirevolution[12], am Abend des glänzendsten 10 Siegestages[13], als jedes Haus eine Festung war, jedes Fenster eine Schanze; — das Volk stürmte die Tuilerien[14]. Selbst Frauen und Kinder befanden sich unter[15] den Kämpfenden; sie drangen in die Gemächer und Säle des Schlosses. Ein armer, halberwachsener Knabe in Lumpen kämpfte mutig unter den 15 älteren Kriegern; tötlich verwundet von mehreren Bajonett= stichen sank er zusammen[16]; das geschah in dem Thronsaale; man legte den Blutenden auf den Thron Frankreichs, wickelte den Samt um seine Wunden; sein Blut strömte auf den könig= lichen Purpur. Das war ein Gemälde! Der prächtige Saal, 20 die kämpfenden Gruppen! Eine zerbrochene Fahne lag auf dem Fußboden, die dreifarbige[17] Flagge wehte über den Bajonetten, und auf dem Throne der arme Knabe mit dem blassen, verklärten Gesicht, die Augen gen[18] Himmel gerichtet, während seine Glieder im Todeskampfe zuckten; seine nackte 25 Brust, seine ärmliche Kleidung, halb bedeckt von dem reichen, *mit silbernen*[19] *Lilien gestickten Samt.* An des Knaben Wiege

war prophezeit: „„Auf Frankreichs Throne wird er sterben!“ „
Das Mutterherz träumte von einem zweiten Napoleon²⁰. —
Meine Strahlen haben den Immortellenkranz²¹ auf seinem
Grabe geküßt; meine Strahlen haben in dieser Nacht die Stirn
⁵ der alten Großmutter geküßt, während sie träumend das Bild
erblickte, welches du hier zeichnen kannst: „„Der arme Knabe
auf dem Throne Frankreichs.“ „

Fünfter Abend.

„In Upsala¹ bin ich gewesen,“ sagte der Mond. „Ich
blickte hinunter² auf die große Ebene mit dem ärmlichen Grase
¹⁰ und den unfruchtbaren Feldern. Ich spiegelte mich in dem
Fyris=Flusse³, während das Dampfboot die Fische in's Schilf
trieb. Unter mir flogen die Wolken und warfen lange
Schatten über die sogenannten⁴ Gräber von Odin, Thor und
Freya. In dem dürftigen Rasen, der die Hügel bekleidet, sind
¹⁵ Namen eingeschnitten. Hier ist kein Denkstein, worin der
Reisende seinen Namen einhauen, keine Felsenwand, worauf er
ihn malen lassen⁵ könnte; deshalb läßt der Besuchende den
Rasen wegstechen. Die nackte Erde blickt in großen Buchstaben
und Namen durch⁶; sie bilden ein Netz über die großen Hügel:
²⁰ eine Unsterblichkeit, welche der neue Rasen bald deckt! Oben
auf dem Hügel stand ein Mann, ein Sänger, er leerte das
Methorn⁷ mit dem breiten, silbernen Rand und lispelte einen

Namen: er bat die Winde, ihn nicht zu verraten, aber ich hörte den Namen; ich kannte ihn[8]; eine Grafenkrone funkelte darüber, und deshalb nannte er ihn nicht laut. Ich lächelte: eine Dichterkrone schmückt ja[9] den seinigen! Der Adel Eleo= norens[10] von Este iſt an Taſſo's Namen geknüpft. Auch weiß ich, wo der Schönheit Roſe[11] blüht!" —

So ſprach der Mond, und zwiſchen uns trat eine Wolke. Mögen keine Wolken den Dichter von der Roſe trennen!

Sechſter Abend.

„Längs dem[1] Strande erſtreckt ſich ein Wald von Fichten und Buchen, ſo friſch und ſo duftend: Hunderte von Nach= tigallen beſuchen ihn jedes Frühjahr. Dicht dabei iſt das Meer, das ewig wechſelnde Meer, und zwiſchen beiden läuft der breite Fahrweg hin[2]. Ein Wagen nach dem andern rollt darüber; ich folge ihnen nicht; mein Auge ruht am liebſten[3] auf einem Punkte. Dort liegt ein Hünengrab[4]. Brombeer= ranken und Schlehdorn wuchern zwiſchen den Steinen. Hier iſt Poeſie in der Natur. Wie glaubſt du wohl[5], daß die Men= ſchen dieſe auffaſſen? Ich will dir erzählen, was ich am vorigen Abend und in der Nacht dort hörte: Zuerſt kamen zwei reiche Gutsbeſitzer gefahren[6]. „„Das[7] ſind herrliche Bäume!"" ſagte der eine. „„Jeder giebt gewiß zehn Fuder Brennholz,"" antwortete der andere. „„Der Winter wird

hart werden; vergangenes Jahr bekamen wir für die[8] Klafter
vierzehn Thaler"" — und fort[9] waren sie. „„Der Weg ist
hier erbärmlich,"" meinte ein anderer Fahrender. „„Daran
sind die verdammten Bäume schuld,"" antwortete sein Nach=
bar; „„hier ist kein Luftzug, der Wind kann nur von der
Seeseite hierher kommen,"" — und sie rollten davon[10]. Auch
der Eilwagen fuhr vorüber[11]. Alle Passagiere[12] schliefen an
diesem schönen Punkt; der Postillion blies ins[13] Horn, aber er
dachte nur: „„Ich blase doch schön. Hier hallt es recht
hübsch; ob es wohl[14] Denen[15] drinnen gefällt?"" Und fort
war der Eilwagen. Alsdann kamen zwei junge Burschen zu
Pferde angesprengt[16]. Da ist Jugend und Champagner im
Blute, dachte ich; sie blickten mit einem Lächeln nach dem moos=
bewachsenen Hügel und dem dichten Gebüsche. „„Hier möchte
ich wohl[17] mit des Müllers Christine ein wenig spazieren
gehen!"" sagte der eine — und fort waren sie.

Die Blumen dufteten sehr stark; jedes Lüftchen schlummerte;
es war, als sei[18] das Meer ein Teil des Himmels, der über das
tiefe Thal gespannt war. Ein Wagen fuhr vorüber[19]; es[20]
saßen sechs Personen darin; vier schliefen, der fünfte dachte
an[21] seinen neuen Sommerrock, der ihm sehr gut stehen müsse;
der sechste wandte sich an den Kutscher und fragte, ob an dem
Steinhaufen etwas Merkwürdiges sei[22]. „„Nein!"" ant=
wortete der Kutscher; „„es ist nur ein Steinhaufen, aber die
Bäume sind merkwürdig."" — „„Wie so?"" „„Ja, das
will ich Ihnen sagen, die[23] sind sehr merkwürdig. Sehen Sie,
wenn im Winter der Schnee sehr hoch liegt und alles verweht

und kein Weg zu sehen ist, dann dienen mir diese Bäume als
Zeichen; nach diesen richte ich mich, um nicht in die See zu
fahren, sehen Sie, deshalb sind die Bäume merkwürdig."
Jetzt kam ein Maler; sein Auge funkelte; er sagte kein Wort,
sondern pfiff; die Nachtigallen schlugen, eine lauter als die an= 5
dere. „„Halt' das Maul!"" rief er und notierte dann ganz
genau alle Farben und Übergänge. „„Blau, lila, dunkelbraun!
Es kann ein schönes Gemälde werden."" Er faßte es auf²⁴
wie der Spiegel ein Bild, und dazu pfiff er einen Marsch von
Rossini²⁵. — Zuletzt kam ein armes Mädchen; sie ruhte auf 10
dem Hünengrabe aus²⁶ und legte ihre Last ab²⁷; das schöne,
blasse Gesicht bog sich lauschend nach dem Walde hin²⁸; ihre
Augen funkelten, sie blickte über die See und den Himmel, die
Hände falteten sich: ich glaube, sie betete ein Vater=unser.
Sie selbst verstand das Gefühl nicht, welches sie durchströmte, 15
aber ich weiß, daß noch nach Jahren diese Minute und die
Natur ringsum weit schöner, ja weit getreuer, als der Maler sie
mit den Farben auf das Papier brachte, ihr²⁹ vor der Erinne=
rung schweben wird. Meine Strahlen folgten ihr, bis das
Morgenrot ihre Stirne küßte."
                                                                      20

Siebenter Abend.

Es¹ hingen schwere Wolken am Himmel, der Mond kam gar
nicht zum Vorschein; ich stand doppelt einsam in meiner kleinen

Kammer und fah hinaus² in die Luft, wo er hätte³ erscheinen
follen. Meine Gedanken flogen weit umher⁴, hinauf zu mei=
nem großen Freunde, der mir jeden Abend so hübsche Ge=
schichten erzählte und mir Bilder zeigte. Ja, was hat der
5 nicht⁵ alles erlebt! Er glitt über die Gewässer der Sündflut⁶,
lächelte gerade so, wie er zu mir herunterblickt, auf Noah's
Arche nieder⁷, und brachte Trost und Kunde von einer neuen
Welt, die hervorblühen würde. Als das Volk Israel's weinend
an Babylon's Flusse⁸ stand, schaute er wehmütig nach den
10 Weiden⁹, wo die Harfen hingen. Als Romeo den Balkon¹⁰
erklomm und der Liebe Weihekuß wie ein Cherub gen¹¹ Himmel
stieg, schwebte der runde Mond, halb zwischen dunkeln Cypressen
versteckt, in der durchsichtigen Luft. Er¹² hat den Helden auf
St. Helena¹³ erblickt, wenn er von dem einsamen Felsen über
15 das Weltmeer schaute, während große Gedanken in seiner Brust
stürmten. Ja, was kann der Mond nicht¹⁴ alles erzählen!
Das Weltleben ist für ihn ein Märchen. Heute sehe ich dich
nicht wieder, alter Freund! Heute kann ich kein Bild der Erin=
nerung an deinen Besuch zeichnen! — Und wie¹⁵ ich träumend
20 in die Wolken blickte, wurde es hell; es war ein Strahl des
Mondes, aber er verschwand wieder; dunkle Wolken zogen vor=
über¹⁶; es war aber doch ein Gruß, ein freundlicher Abendgruß,
vom¹⁷ Monde mir dargebracht.

Achter Abend.

Die Luft war wieder klar; mehrere Abende waren ver=
gangen; der Mond stand im ersten Viertel. Er gab mir auf's
neue die Idee zu einer Skizze; höre, was er mir erzählte:

„Ich folgte dem Polarvogel[1] und dem schwimmenden Wal=
fische nach Grönland's östlicher Küste; unfruchtbare, eisbedeckte 5
Felsen und finstere Wolken umschlingen dort ein Thal, wo
Weidengesträpp und Heidelbeerkraut in reichem Flor standen.
Die duftende Lychnis[2] verbreitete süßen Geruch; mein Licht
war matt, mein Gesicht blaß wie die Nixenblume[3], welche, von
ihrem Stengel losgerissen, wochenlang auf dem Wasser ge= 10
trieben hat. Die Nordlichtkrone[4] brannte; ihr Ring war breit,
und von[5] ihr aus gingen die Strahlen wie wirbelnde Feuer=
säulen über den ganzen Himmel und spielten in grün und rot.
Die in der Nähe Wohnenden versammelten sich zu Tanz und
Lustbarkeit, aber an diese prächtige Erscheinung gewöhnt, wür= 15
digten sie dieselbe kaum eines Blickes. „„Lassen wir[6] nun die
Seelen der Verstorbenen Ball spielen mit den Köpfen der Wal=
rosse!"" dachten sie ihrem Glauben gemäß[7], und hatten nur
Sinn und Augen für Gesang und Tanz. Mitten im Kreise
stand, ohne Pelz, ein Grönländer mit seiner Maultrommel und 20
stimmte einen Gesang an von dem Seehundsfang, und der
Chor antwortete mit: „„Eia! Eia! A!"" und sie sprangen
in ihren weißen Pelzen im Kreise herum[8]; es sah einem Eis=
bären=Ball ähnlich. Die Augen und der Kopf machten die

kühnsten Bewegungen.   Nun begann Gericht und Urteil.   Die=
jenigen, welche sich veruneinigt hatten, traten auf⁹; der Be=
leidigte improvisierte die Fehler seines Gegners, keck und
spottend, alles beim Tanz nach der Trommel¹⁰; der Angeklagte
5 antwortete eben so pfiffig, während die Versammlung lachte
und ihr Urteil fällte.   Die Felsen dröhnten, die Gletscher
krachten, die großen herunterfallenden Massen zerstoben wäh=
rend des Falles; es war eine grönländische, herrliche Sommer=
nacht!—Hundert Schritte entfernt, unter dem offenen Zelte von
10 Fellen, lag ein Kranker; noch strömte das Leben durch sein
warmes Blut, aber doch mußte er sterben, denn er selbst war
davon überzeugt und alle, die rings umher standen, waren es¹¹;
deshalb nähte seine Frau ihn bereits in einen Überzug von
Fellen, damit sie nachher nicht nötig¹² hätte, den Toten zu be=
15 rühren.   Und sie fragte: „„Wünschest du auf dem Felsen in
den¹³ festen Schnee begraben zu werden? Ich werde die Stelle
mit deinem Kajak¹⁴ und deinen Pfeilen schmücken; der Angekok¹⁵
soll über sie wegtanzen. Oder ziehst du vor¹⁶, ins Meer gesenkt
zu werden?"" — „„Ins Meer!"" lispelte er und nickte mit
20 einem wehmütigen Lächeln.   „„Das ist ein angenehmes Som=
merzelt!"" sagte die Frau; „„dort tummeln sich Tausende
von Seehunden, da schläft das Walroß zu deinen Füßen, und
die Jagd ist gefahrlos und lustig!"" Und die Kinder rissen
heulend die ausgespannte Haut von dem Fensterloche, damit der
25 Tote zum Meere geführt werden konnte, zum wogenden Meere,
das ihm im Leben Nahrung gewährte, ihm jetzt im Tode Ruhe
giebt. Die schwimmenden, wie Tag und Nacht wechselnden

Eisberge wurden sein Denkmal. Der Seehund schläft auf der Eisscholle, der Sturmvogel fliegt darüber hinweg[17]."

Neunter Abend.

„Ich kannte eine alte Jungfer," erzählte der Mond; „sie trug jeden Winter einen Überrock von gelbem Atlas; er blieb stets neu; es war ihre einzige Mode. Jeden Sommer trug sie einen und denselben Strohhut und ich glaube, ein und dasselbe blaugraue Kleid.

Nur zu einer alten Freundin quer über die Straße ging sie; in den letzten Jahren that sie auch dies nicht, denn die Freundin war tot. In ihrer Einsamkeit war meine alte Jungfer stets am Fenster geschäftig, vor welchem während des ganzen Sommers hübsche Blumen standen und im Winter herrliche Kresse, auf einen Hutfilz gesät[1]. In dem letztvergangenen Monate sah ich sie nicht mehr am Fenster; aber sie lebte noch, das wußte ich, denn ich hatte sie noch nicht die große Reise antreten sehen, von der sie mit ihrer Freundin so oft sprach. „„Ja!" " pflegte sie dann zu sagen, „„wenn ich einmal sterbe[2], werde ich eine weitere Reise zu machen haben, als während meines ganzen Lebens; sechs Meilen von hier ist unser Familienbegräbnis; dorthin werde[3] ich gebracht, dort werde ich schlafen bei den andern von meiner Verwandtschaft." " Gestern Nacht hielt ein Wagen vor dem Hause; man trug einen Sarg heraus[4]: nur

wußte ich, daß sie gestorben sei[5]. Man legte Stroh um den
Sarg und fuhr davon[6]. Da schlief die stille alte Jungfer, die
in dem letzten Jahre das Haus nicht verlassen hatte. Der
Wagen rollte zum Thore hinaus[7], schnell, als gelte[8] es einer
Spazierfahrt. Auf der Landstraße ging es noch schneller.
Der Kutscher blickte mitunter verstohlen hinter sich: ich glaube,
er fürchtete, sie in ihrem gelben Atlasrocke auf dem Sarge sitzen
zu sehen. Deshalb peitschte er die Pferde unvernünftig, und
hielt dabei die Zügel so straff angezogen, daß die Pferde
schäumten. Sie waren jung und mutig, ein Hase sprang über
den Weg; sie gingen durch[9]. Die alte stille Jungfer, die Jahr
aus Jahr ein sich zu Hause nur in langsamem Kreisgange be=
wegt hatte, fuhr nun, eine Tote[10], über Stock[11] und Stein auf
der offenen Landstraße. Der Sarg, in Strohdecken gehüllt,
flog herab[12] und blieb auf dem Wege liegen, während Pferde,
Kutscher und Wagen in wildem Fluge von dannen jagten.
Die Lerche stieg singend vom Felde auf[13], zwitscherte ihren
Morgengesang über dem Sarg, setzte sich darauf und pickte mit
dem Schnabel in die Strohdecke, als wollte sie sie[14] zerreißen.
Die Lerche erhob sich wieder singend, und ich zog mich zurück[15]
hinter die roten Morgenwolken."

Zehnter Abend.

„Ich will dir ein Bild von Pompeji[1] geben," sagte der Mond.
„Ich war in der Vorstadt[2], in der Straße der Gräber[3], wie sie

sie nennen, wo die schönen Denkmäler stehen, wo vor Zeiten⁴
die jubelnden Jünglinge, Rosen um die Schläfen⁵ mit den schönen
Schwestern der Lais⁶ tanzten.   Jetzt herrschte hier Todenstille ;
deutsche Söldlinge in neapolitanischem Dienste⁷ hielten Wache,
spielten Karte und würfelten ; eine Schar Fremder⁸ von jenseits 5
der Berge⁹ zog in die Stadt ein¹⁰, von¹¹ einer Wache begleitet.
In meinem vollen Lichte wollten sie die aus dem Grabe erstandene
Stadt sehen, und ich zeigte ihnen die Spuren der Wagenräder
in den mit breiten Lavasteinen¹² gepflasterten Straßen, ich
zeigte ihnen die Namen an den Thüren und die noch aushängen= 10
den Schilder ; sie sahen in den kleinen Höfen die Bassins¹³ der
Springbrunnen, mit Muscheln geschmückt, aber kein Wasser=
strahl stieg empor¹⁴, keine Lieder ertönten aus den reichgemalten
Gemächern, wo der eherne¹⁵ Hund die Thür bewachte.

Es war die Stadt der Toten ; nur der Vesuv donnerte noch 15
seine ewige Hymne, von welcher jeder einzelne Vers von¹⁶ den
Menschen ein neuer Ausbruch¹⁷ genannt wird.   Wir gingen
nach dem Tempel der Venus¹⁸, aus schneeweißem Marmor
aufgeführt, mit seinem Hochaltar vor der breiten Treppe und
mit frisch emporgeschossenen Trauerweiden¹⁹ zwischen den Säu= 20
len ; die Luft war durchsichtig und blau, den Hintergrund bil=
dete der schwarze Vesuv, aus dem das Feuer emporstieg wie
der Stamm der Pinie²⁰.   Darüber lag die Rauchwolke in der
Stille der Nacht, wie die Krone der Pinie, aber in blutigroter
Beleuchtung.   Unter²¹ der Gesellschaft war eine Sängerin, 25
eine wirkliche und große Sängerin, ich bin Zeuge der ihr ge=
brachten Huldigungen in Europa's größten Städten gewesen.

Als sie sich dem tragischen [22] Theater nahten, nahmen sie alle
Platz auf den steinernen Stufen des Amphitheaters ; ein kleiner
Teil desselben wurde wieder gefüllt, wie vor [23] Jahrtausenden.
Die Bühne stand noch unverändert mit den gemauerten Coulissen
und den beiden Bogen im Hintergrunde, durch welche man die=
selbe Dekoration [24] wie damals schaut, die Natur selbst, die
Berge zwischen Sorrento [25] und Amalfi.   Die Sängerin bestieg
scherzend die Bühne des Altertums und sang.   Der Ort be=
geisterte sie; ich mußte an das wilde Pferd Arabien's denken,
wenn es schnaubend die Mähne sträubt und von dannen jagt,
es war dieselbe Leichtigkeit und Sicherheit; ich mußte an die
schmerzerfüllte [26] Mutter unter Golgatha's Kreuz denken, es war
derselbe tief gefühlte Schmerz.   Und ringsum ertönte, wie vor [27]
tausend Jahren, Beifall und Jubel: „ „Glückliche [28], vom
Himmel Begabte!" " jubelten alle.   Fünf Minuten später war
die Bühne leer, die Gesellschaft verschwunden, keine Töne
wurden mehr gehört, — alle fort [29], aber die Ruinen standen
unverändert, wie sie noch nach Jahrhunderten stehen werden,
und niemand weiß dann etwas von dem Beifalle des Augen=
blicks und von der schönen Sängerin, von ihren Tönen, ihrem
Lächeln; alles ist [30] vergessen und vorüber, selbst für mich wird
diese Stunde ein entschwundener Moment sein."

Elfter Abend.

„Ich blickte in die Fenster eines Redacteurs,[1]" sagte der
Mond, „es war irgendwo in Deutschland, ich sah schöne Möbel,
viele Bücher und ein Chaos von Zeitungsblättern. Mehrere
junge Männer waren zugegen, der Redacteur selbst[2] stand an
seinem Pulte, zwei kleine Bücher, beide von jungen Schrift- 5
stellern, sollten[3] angekündigt werden. „„Das eine ist mir zu-
gestellt worden,"" sagte er, „„ich habe es noch nicht gelesen, aber
es ist schön ausgestattet; was halten Sie von dem Inhalte?""

„„Oh!"" sagte der eine, er war selbst ein Dichter, — „„der[4]
ist schön, freilich etwas breit, aber lieber Gott![5] der Verfasser 10
ist noch jung; die Verse könnten[6] allerdings besser sein. Die
Gedanken sind gesund, freilich sind darunter viele Gemein-
plätze! Doch was soll man sagen? Man kann nicht immer
etwas Neues erfinden. Sie können ihn immerhin loben!
Daß etwas Großes aus ihm wird, glaube ich nicht. Aber er 15
ist belesen, ein vorzüglicher Orientalist, hat ein gesundes Urteil.
Er ist es,[7] der die hübsche Recension meiner „„Phantasie über
das häusliche Leben"" geschrieben hat, man muß nachsichtig
gegen den jungen Mann sein.""

„„Aber er ist ja[8] ein wahres Pferd[9]!"" meinte einer der 20
andern anwesenden Herren. „„Nichts ist in der Poesie schreck-
licher, als die Mittelmäßigkeit, diese überschreitet er keinesfalls.""

„„Der arme Teufel[10]!"" sagte der dritte, „„und seine Tante

ist doch so glücklich über ihn; sie ist es[11], Herr[12] Redacteur, die
so viele Subskribenten auf Ihre letzte Übersetzung gesammelt
hat.““   „„Die gute Frau! Ja, ich habe das Buch kurz ange=
zeigt. Unverkennbares Talent! Eine willkommene Gabe! Eine
5 Blume im Garten der Poesie: hübsch ausgestattet u. s. w. Aber
das andere Buch, — der Verfasser will[13] wahrscheinlich, daß
ich es kaufen soll! — Ich höre, es wird gelobt. Genie[14] hat
er! Glauben Sie nicht auch?““

„„Ja, die ganze Welt sagt es,““ antwortete der Dichter,
10 „„aber es ist etwas wild ausgefallen. Besonders die Inter=
punktion ist genial[15]!““

„„Es wird gut für ihn sein, wenn man ihn ein wenig durch=
hechelt und ärgert, sonst bekommt er eine zu große Meinung von
sich selbst.““

15 „„Aber das wäre[16] unbillig,““ äußerte der vierte, „„wir wollen
nicht an den kleinen Fehlern mäkeln, sondern über das viele
vorhandene Gute uns freuen, er sticht sie doch alle aus[17]!““
„„Mit nichten! Wenn er wirklich ein echtes Genie ist, so wird
er auch die scharfe Lauge vertragen. Es giebt[18] Leute genug,
20 die ihn loben; machen wir[19] ihn nicht ganz verrückt!““

„„Unverkennbares Talent!““ schrieb der Redacteur hin[20],
„„die gewöhnlichen Nachläßigkeiten; daß er auch unglückliche
Verse schreiben kann[21], sieht man auf Pagina 25, wo sich zwei
Hiaten[22] vorfinden. Studium der Alten wird empfohlen
25 u. s. w.““—„„Ich entfernte mich,““ sagte der Mond, „und blickte
durch die Fenster in dem Hause der Tante; da saß der gefeierte
*Dichter, der zahme, ihm huldigten alle Eingeladenen, und er war
glücklich.*

Ich suchte auch den andern Dichter auf, den wilden; er be=
fand sich gleichfalls in großer Gesellschaft bei seinem Beschützer,
wo man das Buch des zahmen Dichters besprach. „„Ich werde
auch das Ihrige lesen!"" sagte der Mäcen²³, „„aber ehrlich ge=
sprochen²⁴, Sie wissen, daß ich Ihnen meine Meinung nie vor= 5
enthalte, ich erwarte nicht viel davon²⁵, Sie sind viel zu wild,
viel zu phantastisch. — Aber das muß man Ihnen lassen²⁶, als
Mensch sind Sie sehr achtungswert!"" Ein junges Mädchen
saß in einem Winkel und las in einem Buche:

> In den Staub²⁷ des Talentes Glorie, 10
> Alltägliches aber macht Glück;
> Zwar eine alte Historie,
> Doch täglich spielt das Stück."

Zwölfter Abend.

„Ich glitt über die Lüneburger Heide¹," sagte der Mond;
„eine einsame Hütte lag am Wege, einige ärmliche Büsche stan= 15
den dabei und eine Nachtigall, die sich verirrt hatte, schlug².
In der Kälte der Nacht mußte sie sterben; es war ihr Ab=
schiedsgesang, welchen ich hörte. Die Morgenröte schimmerte.
Ich sah eine Karawane auswandernder Bauernfamilien, die nach
Hamburg wollten³, um mit einem Schiffe Amerika zu erreichen, 20
wo ihnen⁴ das Glück, das geträumte, blühen würde⁵. Die
Mütter trugen die kleinen Kinder auf dem Rücken, die größere

trippelten nebenher, ein elendes Pferd zog einen Karren mit
wenigem Hausgeräte. Der kalte Wind sauste, deshalb
schmiegte das kleine Mädchen sich dichter an seine[6] Mutter,
die, zu meiner abnehmenden[7] Scheibe emporblickend, an[8] ihre
bittere Not daheim dachte und an die schweren Abgaben, welche
sie nicht hatten erschwingen können. Und so dachte die ganze
Karawane; die rote Morgendämmerung leuchtete deshalb als[9]
ein Evangelium von der Sonne des Glücks, die ihnen aufgehen
würde[10]; sie hörten die sterbende Nachtigall schlagen, sie war
kein falscher Prophet, sondern ein Vorbote des Glücks. Der
Wind sauste, daher verstanden sie ihren Gesang nicht: „„Fahret
getrost über das Meer! Die weite Überfahrt hast du ja[11] be-
zahlt mit allem, was dein war, arm und hilflos sollst du dein
Land Kanaan[12] betreten. Du mußt dich[13], deine Frau, deine
Kinder verkaufen. Doch lange sollen eure Leiden nicht währen.
Hinter dem breiten, duftenden Blatte[14] lauert die Göttin des
Todes, ihr bewillkommnender Kuß haucht tötende Fieber in dein
Blut. Fahre hin[15]! fahre hin über die schwellenden Wogen!““
— Und die Karawane horchte freudig dem Gesange der Nachtigall, denn er verkündete ja[16] Glück. Der Tag brach durch die
lichten Wolken, Landleute gingen über die Heide zur Kirche;
die schwarzgekleideten Frauen mit ihrem weißen Kopfputze
schienen[17] wie Geister aus den alten Kirchengemälden heraus-
getreten. Ringsum die weite tote Fläche[18], ringsum das welke
braune Heidekraut, schwarze, abgesengte Ebenen zwischen weißen
Sandhügeln. Die Frauen trugen ihr Gesangbuch und wan-
derten zur Kirche. O! betet! Betet für die, die zum Grabe
andern, jenseits des wogenden Meeres!"

Dreizehnter Abend.

„Ich kenne einen Polichinell[1]," sagte der Mond, „das Publikum jubelt, sobald es ihn erblickt, jede seiner Bewegungen wird komisch, jede versetzt das ganze Haus in lautes Gelächter, und doch ist nichts darin berechnet, es ist wahre Natur. Als er noch als kleiner Junge mit den Knaben herumsprang, war er schon Polichinell, die Natur hatte ihn dazu bestimmt und mit einem Höcker auf dem Rücken und einem Höcker auf der Brust versehen; sein Inneres dagegen, das Geistige, war reich ausgestattet. An Tiefe des Gefühls, an Elasticität des Geistes übertraf ihn niemand. Das Theater war die Welt seiner Ideale. Hätte[2] er einen schlanken und wohlgebauten Körper gehabt, so wäre[3] er der erste Tragiker jeder Bühne geworden, das Heroische, das Große erfüllte seine Seele, und doch mußte er Polichinell werden. Selbst sein Schmerz und seine Melancholie vermehrten die komische Trockenheit seines scharfgezeichneten Gesichts und erregten das Gelächter des zahlreichen Publikums, welches seinem Liebling Beifall spendete! Die liebliche Columbine[4] war zwar freundlich und gut gegen ihn, wollte aber doch am liebsten Harlekin[5] heiraten; es wäre[6] doch gar zu lächerlich gewesen, wenn in der Wirklichkeit die Schönheit[7] und die Häßlichkeit[8] sich verbunden hätten.

Wenn Polichinell recht verstimmt war, vermochte sie allein ihm ein Lächeln, ja sogar ein herzliches Lachen abzuzwingen; zuerst war[10] sie mit ihm melancholisch, dann etwas ruhiger, zuletzt aber von Heiterkeit erfüllt.   „„Ich weiß recht wohl, was Ihnen fehlt!"" sagte sie, „„ja! es ist die Liebe,"" — und er mußte lachen.   „„Ich und Liebe"" rief er, „„das würde sich drollig ausnehmen! Wie das Publikum applaudieren würde!""

5 — „„Gewiß, es ist die Liebe,"" fuhr sie fort¹¹ und fügte mit komischem Pathos hinzu¹² : „„Ich bin es¹³, die Sie lieben!"" So etwas mag man wohl sagen, wenn man weiß, daß keine Rede davon sein kann. — Der Polichinell sprang auch lachend in die Höhe, nun war die Melancholie vergessen. — Und doch hatte sie

10 nur die Wahrheit gesprochen; er liebte sie, liebte sie heiß, wie er das Erhabene und Große in der Kunst liebte! An ihrem Hochzeitstage¹⁴ war er die lustigste Figur, in der Nacht aber weinte er; hätte¹⁵ das Publikum das verzerrte Gesicht gesehen, es¹⁶ würde applaudiert haben. — In diesen Tagen starb Colum=

15 bine; am Begräbnistage wurde von Harlekin nicht verlangt, daß er sich auf den Brettern¹⁷ zeigen sollte, er war ja¹⁸ ein be= trübter Witwer.   Der Direktor mußte etwas recht Lustiges auf= führen lassen, damit das Publikum nicht gar zu sehr die liebliche Columbine und den leichten Harlekin vermißte, deshalb mußte

20 Polichinell doppelt ausgelassen sein, er tanzte und sprang mit Verzweiflung im Herzen, es wurde applaudiert und gejauchzt : bravo! bravissimo!¹⁹ Polichinell wurde herausgerufen.   O! er war unvergleichlich. — — Gestern Nacht wanderte der kleine Unhold allein zur Stadt hinaus²⁰ nach dem einsamen Gottes=

25 acker²¹.   Der Blumenkranz auf Columbinen's Grabe war schon verwelkt; dort setzte er sich nieder²², es war zum malen, den Kopf²³ auf die Hände gestützt, die Augen nach mir gewandt;

er nahm sich aus²⁴ wie ein Monument, ein Polichinell auf dem Grabe, eigentümlich und komisch! Hätte²⁵ das Publikum seinen Liebling gesehen, gewiß würde es applaudiert haben: Bravo, Pulcinella²⁶, bravo bravissimo!"

Vierzehnter Abend.

Höre was der Mond mir erzählt! „Ich habe den Kadetten Offizier werden und sich zum ersten mal in seine prächtige Uniform kleiden sehen: ich habe das junge Mädchen in ihrem Brautstaate gesehen und des Fürsten junge Braut¹ glücklich in ihrem Brautanzuge; aber nie habe ich eine Seligkeit erblickt ähnlich der² eines kleinen vierjährigen Mädchens, welches³ ich heute Abend beobachtete. Sie hatte ein neues blaues Kleid erhalten und einen neuen Rosa=Hut; der Staat war eben ange= legt und alle riefen nach⁴ Licht, denn des Mondes Strahlen, die durch das Fenster drangen, waren nicht hell genug, ganz andere Lichter mußten angebrannt werden. Da stand das kleine Mädchen steif wie eine Puppe, die Arme ängstlich von dem Kleide ab⁵ ausstreckend, die Finger weit auseinander gespreizt. O welche Seligkeit strahlte aus ihren Augen, aus ihrem ganzen Gesicht! „„Morgen sollst du in dem Kleide aus= gehen!"" sagte die Mutter, und die Kleine blickte auf⁶ zu ihrem Hut und wieder nieder zu ihrem Kleide und lächelte selig. „„Mutter!"" rief sie, „„was werden wohl⁷ die kleinen Hündchen denken, wenn sie mich in diesem Staate erblicken?"" — "

Fünfzehnter Abend.

"Ich habe," sagte der Mond, "dir von Pompeji, dieser Leiche einer Stadt, in der Reihe der lebendigen Städte ausgestellt, er= zählt; ich kenne eine[1] andere noch seltsamere, sie[2] ist keine Leiche, aber das Gespenst einer Stadt. Überall, wo die
5 Strahlen der Springbrunnen in Marmorbecken plätschern, kommt es mir vor[3], als hörte[4] ich das Märchen von der schwim= menden Stadt. Ja, der Strahl des Wassers mag von ihr[5] erzählen, die Wellen des Strandes mögen von ihr singen! Über der Fläche des Meeres ruht oft ein Nebel, das ist ihr
10 Wittwenschleier[6]; der Bräutigam[7] des Meeres ist tot, sein Schloß und seine Stadt ist sein Mausoleum[8]! Kennst du diese Stadt? Nie hörte[9] sie das Rollen der Räder oder den Huf= schlag des Pferdes in ihren Straßen, dort schwimmt nur der Fisch herum[10], und gespensterhaft fliegt die schwarze Gondel[11]
15 über das grüne Wasser. Ich will," sagte der Mond, "dir das Forum[12] der Stadt, den größten Platz derselben, zeigen, und du wirst dich in die Stadt der Märchen versetzt glauben. Das Gras wuchert zwischen den breiten Fliesen[13], und in der Mor= gendämmerung flattern Tausende von Tauben um den frei=
20 stehenden[14], hohen Turm herum[15]. Auf drei Seiten bist du von[16] Bogengängen umgeben. Unter ihnen sitzt still der Türke mit seiner langen Pfeife, der schöne Griechenknabe lehnt sich an[17] die Säule und betrachtet die aufgerichteten Trophäen, die hohen Masten, Andenken an[18] die verschwundene Macht[19].

Die Flaggen hängen gleich Trauerflor herab[20]. Ein Mädchen ruht dort aus[21], die schweren Eimer, mit Wasser gefüllt, hat sie hingesetzt, das Joch[22], an welchem sie dieselben getragen hat, ruht auf einer ihrer Schultern, sie lehnt sich an den Siegesmast. Es ist kein Feenschloß, sondern eine Kirche[23], die du vor dir erblickst, die vergoldeten Kuppeln, die glänzenden Kugeln ringsum glänzen in meinem Lichte: die prächtigen ehernen[24] Rosse dort oben haben Reisen gemacht, wie das eherne Pferd[25] im Märchen, sie sind erst hierher, dann fort von hier und wieder hierher gereist. Siehst du die bunte Pracht[26] der Mauern und der Fenster? Es hat das Ansehen[27], als ob das Genie den Launen eines Kindes nachgegeben hätte[28], indem es diesen seltsamen Tempel schmückte. Siehst du auf der Säule den geflügelten[29] Löwen? Das Gold glänzt noch, die Flügel aber sind gebunden, der Löwe ist tot, denn der König des Meeres ist tot, die großen Hallen stehen veröbet, und wo früher die herrlichsten Gemälde prangten, scheint jetzt die nackte Mauer durch[30]. Der Lazzarone[31] schläft unter dem Bogengange, dessen Fußboden früher nur der vornehmste Adel betreten durfte. Aus dem tiefen Brunnen[32] oder auch vielleicht aus den Gefängnissen[33] bei der Seufzerbrücke[34] tönt Jammer, wie zu der Zeit, als das Tambourin[35] aus den bunten Gondeln erscholl, als der Brautring von dem glänzenden Bucentoro[36] zur Adria hinunterflog, zur Adria, der Königin der Meere. Adria! Hülle dich in Nebel! Laß den Witwenschleier deinen Busen verhüllen, hänge ihn über das Mausoleum deines Bräutigams: das marmorne gespenstige Venedig!"

Sechzehnter Abend.

„Ich sah auf ein großes Theater herab[1]," sagte der Mond.
„Das Haus war gedrängt voll, denn ein neuer Schauspieler
debütierte; mein Strahl glitt über ein kleines Fenster in der
Mauer, ein geschminktes Gesicht drückte die Stirn gegen die
5 Scheiben; es war der Held des Abends.   Der ritterliche Bart
kräuselte sich um das Kinn, aber in des Mannes Augen standen
Thränen, denn er war ausgepfiffen worden, und zwar mit
Grund.   Der arme Stümper! Aber Stümper dürfen im Reiche
der Kunst nicht gelitten werden.   Er besaß ein tiefes Gefühl
10 und liebte seine Kunst mit Begeisterung, sie aber liebte ihn
nicht. — — Des Regisseurs[2] Klingel ertönte; „„keck und
mutig,"" so stand in der Rolle, „„tritt der Held heraus[3]"" —
heraus mußte[4] er vor ein Publikum, dem er zum Gelächter[5]
geworden[6]. — — Als das Stück zu Ende war, sah ich eine
15 Gestalt in einen Mantel gehüllt sich die Treppe hinunter=
schleichen, er[7] war es, der vernichtete Ritter des Abends; die
Maschinisten zischelten, ich folgte dem Sünder nach Hause in
seine Kammer.   Sich erhängen ist ein unschöner Tod, und Gift
hat man nicht immer bei der Hand; ich weiß es, an[8] beides
20 dachte er.   Ich sah, wie er das bleiche Antlitz im Spiegel be=
trachtete mit halb zugemachten Augen, um zu sehen, ob er sich
wohl als Leiche gut ausnähme[9].   Der Mensch kann sehr un=
glücklich und dennoch sehr affektiert sein.   Er dachte an den
Tod, an Selbstmord, ich glaube, er beweinte sich selbst, — er

weinte bitterlich, und wenn man sich recht ausgeweint hat, wird man kein Selbstmörder. Ein ganzes Jahr ist seit jener Zeit verstrichen. Es wurde wieder Komödie gespielt, aber auf einem kleinen Theater, von einer armen herumziehenden Truppe; ich sah wieder das bekannte Gesicht, die geschminkten Wangen, den [5] gekräuselten Bart.

Er blickte wieder zu mir empor [10] und lächelte — und gleichwohl war er kaum vor [11] einer Minute ausgepfiffen worden, auf einem elenden Theater und von [12] einem jämmerlichen Publikum! Heute Abend fuhr ein ärmlicher Leichenwagen aus dem [10] Thore, niemand folgte ihm. Es war ein Selbstmörder, unser geschminkter ausgepfiffener Held. Der Kutscher des Leichenwagens war der einzige Begleiter, niemand folgte, niemand weiter [13] als der Mond. Im Winkel an der Kirchhofsmauer wurde der Selbstmörder begraben, die Brennesseln werden bald [15] über seinem Grabe wuchern, der Totengräber wird Dornen und Unkraut von den Gräbern der andern darauf werfen."

Siebzehnter Abend.

„Von Rom komme ich," sagte der Mond, „dort mitten in der Stadt auf einem der sieben Hügel liegen die Ruinen der Kaiserburg [1]; der wilde Feigenbaum wächst in den Spalten der Mauer [20] und bedeckt deren Nacktheit mit seinen breiten graugrünen Blättern; zwischen Schutthaufen tritt der Esel auf grüne Lor-

beersträuche und freut sich der unfruchtbaren Disteln. Von
hier aus, wo sonst die Adler[2] Roma's ausflogen, kamen[3], sahen
und siegten, führt ein Eingang durch ein kleines, ärmliches
Haus, aus Lehm zusammengefügt, zwischen zwei Marmorsäulen;
die Weinranke hängt wie eine Trauerguirlande über dem schiefen
Fenster; eine alte Frau mit ihrer kleinen Enkelin wohnt darin,
sie herrschen jetzt in der Kaiserburg und zeigen den Fremden die
versunkenen Schätze. Von dem reichen Thronsaale steht nur
noch eine nackte Wand, eine schwarze Cypresse zeigt mit ihrem
langen Schatten auf die Stelle, wo einst der Thron stand.
Der Schutt liegt ellenhoch über dem zertrümmerten Fußboden;
das kleine Mädchen, jetzt die Tochter der Kaiserburg, sitzt oft
dort auf ihrem Schemel, wenn die Abendglocken läuten. Das
Schlüsselloch in der Thür dicht daneben nennt sie ihr Erkerfen=
ster; durch dieses kann sie das halbe Rom überblicken bis an
die mächtige Kuppel der Peterskirche[4]. Ruhe herrschte, wie
stets, so auch diesen Abend; unten in meinem vollen, hellen
Lichte kam die kleine Enkelin. Auf ihrem Kopfe trug sie ein
irdenes Gefäß von antiker Form, mit Wasser gefüllt. Ihre
Füße waren nackt, der kurze Rock und die Ärmel des kleinen
Hembes zerrissen; ich küßte ihre feinen runden Schultern, ihre
dunklen Augen und die schwarzen, glänzenden Haare. Sie stieg
die Treppe hinauf[5]; diese war steil, von marmornen Bruch=
stücken und einem zertrümmerten Kapitäl[6] zusammengefügt.
Die buntfarbigen Eidechsen fuhren scheu an ihren Füßen vor=
über[7], sie aber erschrak nicht; schon hob sie die Hand, um die
Hausklingel zu ziehen: eine an einen Bindfaden befestigte

Hafenpfote bildete den Klingelzug der Kaiserburg. Sie hielt
einen Augenblick an[8], woran[9] dachte sie wohl? Vielleicht an
das schöne Christkind, in Gold und Silber gekleidet, welches
unten in der Kapelle hing, wo die silbernen Leuchter strahlten,
wo ihre kleinen Freundinnen den Gesang anstimmten, den auch 5
sie kannte? Ich weiß es nicht. Sie machte wieder eine Be=
wegung, strauchelte, der irdene Krug fiel ihr[10] vom Kopfe und
zerbrach auf den Marmorfliesen[11]. Sie brach in Thränen aus[12],
die schöne Tochter der Kaiserburg weinte um[13] den geringen,
zerbrochenen Krug; mit nackten Füßen stand sie da[14] und weinte, 10
und wagte nicht, den Bindfaden zu ziehen, den Klingelzug der
Kaiserburg!"

Achtzehnter Abend.

Es war[1] mehr als vierzehn[2] Tage her, daß der Mond nicht
geschienen hatte, jetzt stand er rund und hell da[3] über den lang=
sam ziehenden Wolken. Höre, was der Mond mir erzählte: 15
"Von einer Stadt in Fezzan[4] aus folgte ich einer Karawane;
vor der Sandwüste auf einer der Salzebenen, die wie eine Eis=
fläche glänzte und nur stellenweise mit leichtem Flugsande be=
deckt war, wurde halt gemacht. Der Älteste — die Wasser=
flasche hing an seinem Gürtel, auf seinem Kopfe lag ein Säck= 20
chen mit ungesäuertem[5] Brote — malte mit seinem Stabe ein
Viereck in den Sand und schrieb darein einige Worte aus dem

Koran⁶; über bie geweihte Stelle zog bie ganze Karawane hin⁷. Ein junger Kaufmann, ein Kind ber Sonne⁸, ich erkannte es an⁹ seinem Auge unb ben schönen Formen, ritt gebankenvoll auf seinem weißen, schnaubenben Pferbe. Dachte er vielleicht an¹⁰ sein schönes, junges Weib? Es war¹¹ nur zwei Tage her, baß bas Kamel, mit Fellen unb kostbaren Shawls geschmückt, sie, bie herrliche Braut um bie Mauer ber Stabt getragen¹²; Trommeln unb Schalmeien ertönten, bie Weiber sangen, rings um bas Kamel hallten bie Freubenschüsse, ber Bräutigam feuerte bie meisten ab¹³, unb jetzt — zog er mit ber Karawane burch bie Wüste. Viele Nächte folgte ich ihr¹⁴, ich sah sie¹⁵ ruhen an ben Brunnen zwischen verkümmerten Palmen, sie stachen bas Messer in bie Brust bes gestürzten Kamels unb rösteten sein Fleisch am Feuer. Meine Strahlen kühlten ben glühenben Sanb, sie zeigten ihnen bie schwarzen Felsenblöcke, bie toten Inseln in bem ungeheuern Sanbmeere; keine feinblichen Stämme begegneten ihnen auf Wegen ohne Spur, keine Stürme erhoben sich, keine Sanbsäulen zogen verberbenbringenb über bie Karawane hinweg¹⁶. Zu Hause betete bie schöne Frau für ben Mann unb Vater. „„Sinb sie tot?"" fragte sie mein golbenes Horn. „„Sinb sie tot?"" fragte sie meine strahlenbe volle Scheibe. Jetzt liegt bie Wüste hinter ihnen; heute Abenb sitzen sie unter ben hohen Palmen, von bem Kranich mit seinen ellenlangen Flügeln umflattert; ber Pelikan betrachtet sie von ben Zweigen ber Mimosen¹⁷ herab¹⁸; bas üppig wuchernbe Gesträuch ist unter ben plumpen Füßen ber Elefanten niebergetreten. Eine Negerschar kehrt aus bem Innern bes Lanbes von einem

Markte zurück[19], die Weiber, mit kupfernen Knöpfen in ihrem
schwarzen Haar und mit indigofarbenen Röcken geputzt, treiben
die schwerbeladenen Ochsen, auf deren Rücken die nackten schwarzen Kinder schlafen. Ein Neger führt an der Leine einen jungen Löwen, den er gekauft hat. Sie nähern sich der Kara- 5
wane; der junge Kaufmann sitzt unbeweglich und schweigend,
und denkt an[20] seine schöne Frau, träumt im Lande der Schwarzen von seiner weißen, duftenden Blume jenseits der Wüste;
er hebt seinen Kopf — ?—" eine Wolke trat vor den Mond und
dann noch eine Wolke. Ich erfuhr diesen Abend nichts weiter. 10

Neunzehnter Abend.

„Ich sah ein kleines Mädchen weinen," sagte der Mond, „sie
weinte über[1] die Bosheit der Welt. Sie hatte eine herrliche
Puppe geschenkt bekommen[2]. O! das war eine Puppe, so
schön und zart! Sie war nicht geschaffen für die Leiden dieser
Welt. Aber die Brüder des kleinen Mädchens, die großen, 15
ungezogenen Jungen, hatten die Puppe hoch oben auf einen großen Baum im Garten gesetzt und waren dann davongelaufen.

Das kleine Mädchen konnte die Puppe nicht erreichen, ihr
nicht herunterhelfen, und deshalb weinte es[3]: die Puppe weinte
ganz bestimmt auch mit[4], sie streckte die Arme zwischen den grü- 20
nen Zweigen herab[5] und sah ganz unglücklich aus[6]. Ja, das
sind die Leiden der Welt, von denen[7] Mama so oft gesprochen[8].

Ach, die arme Puppe! Es fing[9] schon an dunkel zu werden,
und wenn nun erst die Nacht vollends einbräche[10]! Sollte sie[11]
draußen auf dem Baume ganz allein die ganze Nacht sitzen?
Nein! Das konnte das kleine Mädchen nicht über das Herz
5   bringen. „„Ich will bei dir bleiben!““ sagte sie, obwohl ihr
durchaus nicht wohl dabei zu Mute war. Es kam ihr schon
vor[12], als sähe[13] sie ganz deutlich die kleinen Kobolde mit ihren
hohen spitzen Mützen im Gebüsche kauern, und weiter hinten in
dem finstern Gange tanzten lange Gespenster; sie kamen näher
10   und näher und streckten die Hände gegen den Baum aus[14], wo
die Puppe saß, sie lachten höhnisch, mit den Fingern nach ihr
zeigend. Ach, wie bange war dem kleinen Mädchen! „„Aber
wenn man keine Sünde begangen hat,““ dachte sie, „„kann das
Böse Einem nichts zu leide thun. Ob ich wohl[15] eine Sünde
15   begangen habe?““ Und sie dachte nach[16]. „„Ach ja! Ich
habe die arme Ente mit dem roten Lappen am Beine aus=
gelacht, sie hinkte so possierlich, deshalb mußte ich lachen, aber
es ist eine Sünde, über die Tiere zu lachen.““ Und sie blickte
zur Puppe auf[17]. „„Hast du über die Tiere gelacht?““ fragte
20   sie, und es sah aus[18], als schüttelte die Puppe mit[19] dem Kopfe.“

Zwanzigster Abend.

„Ich blickte auf Tirol herab[1],“ sagte der Mond, „ich ließ die
dunklen Tannen große Schlagschatten auf die Felsen werfen.

Ich betrachtete den heiligen Chriſtoph[2], das Jeſuskind auf ſei=
nen Schultern tragend, wie ſie dort auf die Mauern der Häuſer
gemalt ſind, in koloſſaler Größe vom Grunde auf bis an das
Dach. Der heilige Florian[3] goß Waſſer auf das brennende Haus
und Chriſtus hing blutend an dem großen Kreuz am Wege. Für [5]
das neue Geſchlecht ſind das alte Bilder, ich dagegen habe ge=
ſehen, wie ſie errichtet wurden, wie eins dem andern folgte.
Auf dem Abhange hoch oben hängt, einem Schwalbenneſte
gleich[4], ein einſames Nonnenkloſter; zwei Schweſtern ſtanden
oben im Turme und läuteten; ſie waren beide jung, deshalb [10]
flog ihr Blick über die Berge in die Welt hinaus[5]. Ein Reiſe=
wagen fuhr unten vorbei[6], das Poſthorn erklang, die armen
Nonnen hefteten mit verwandten Gedanken ihren Blick auf den
Wagen, in dem Auge der jüngern glänzte eine Thräne. — Und
das Horn erklang ſchwächer und ſchwächer, die Glocken des [15]
Kloſters übertäubten ſeine hinſterbenden Töne."

Einundzwanzigſter Abend.

Höre, was der Mond erzählte. „Vor[1] mehreren Jahren, es
war in Kopenhagen[2], blickte ich durch das Fenſter einer ärm=
lichen Stube. Der Vater und die Mutter ſchliefen, der kleine
Sohn ſchlief aber nicht. Ich ſah die Bettvorhänge von geblüm= [20]
tem Kattun ſich bewegen und das Kind hervorblicken. Zuerſt
dachte ich, daß es[3] nach der großen Wanduhr ſähe[4], die gar zu

schön rot und grün bemalt war; oben saß ein Kuckuck[5], unten
hingen die schweren Bleigewichte und der Perpendikel mit der
blankpolierten Messingscheibe ging hin und her, tick, tack; doch
nicht die Uhr betrachtete er, nein, es war das Spinnrad seiner
5 Mutter, das gerade unter der Uhr stand. Das war von allen
des Knaben liebstes Stück[6], er durfte es aber nicht anrühren,
sonst wurde ihm[7] auf die Finger geklopft. Ganze Stunden
hindurch, wenn die Mutter spann, konnte er ruhig dabei sitzen
und die schnurrende Spule und das sich drehende Rad betrach=
10 ten, und dabei machte er sich nun seine Gedanken. Ach! wenn er
doch auch das Spinnrad drehen dürfte[8]. Der Vater und die
Mutter schliefen, er sah sie an[9], sah das Spinnrad an[10] und
kurz darauf guckte ein kleiner nackter Fuß zum Bette heraus[11],
und dann noch einer, und dann zwei Beinchen. Da stand er.
15 Er schaute sich nochmals um[12], ob Vater und Mutter auch noch
schliefen; ja, sie schliefen; und nun schlich er leise, ganz leise,
in seinem kleinen kurzen Hembe zu dem Spinnrade hin[13] und
fing an[14] zu spinnen. Die Schnur flog vom Rade ab[15], das
Rad lief noch schneller. Ich küßte seine blonden Haare und
20 seine blauen Augen, es war ein liebliches Bild. In diesem
Augenblick erwachte die Mutter, der Vorhang bewegte sich, sie
sah hervor[16] und meinte einen Kobold oder ein anderes kleines
Gespenst zu erblicken. „„Im Namen Jesu[17]!"" rief sie und
stieß ängstlich ihren Mann in die Seite; er schlug die Augen
25 auf[18], rieb sie mit den Händen und blickte nach dem kleinen flin=
ken Burschen. „„Aber das ist ja[19] Bertel[20]!"" rief er. —
Und mein Auge verließ die ärmliche Stube, ich muß ja so vie-

les sehen! In demselben Augenblick schaute ich in die Säle des Vatikans²¹, wo die Marmorgötter stehen. Ich bestrahlte die Laokoon=Gruppe²²; der Stein schien zu seufzen; ich drückte einen stillen Kuß auf die Brüste der Musen²³, es kam mir vor²⁴, als höben²⁵ sie sich. Doch am längsten weilten meine Strahlen bei der Nilgruppe²⁶, bei dem kolossalen Gott. An die Sphinx²⁷ sich lehnend, liegt er gedankenvoll und träumend da²⁸, als dächte²⁹ er an³⁰ die dahinrollenden Jahrhunderte; die kleinen Liebesgötter treiben mit den Krokodilen ihr Spiel. In dem Füllhorne saß mit gekreuzten Armen ein ganz kleiner Amor, den großen ernsten Flußgott betrachtend, ein treues Bild³¹ des klei=nen Knaben am Spinnrade, es³² waren ganz dieselben Züge³³; lebendig und reizend stand hier das kleine Marmorbild, und doch hat sich das Rad des Jahres mehr als tausend Mal gedreht seit der Zeit, wo es aus dem Steine hervorsprang. Eben so oft, als der Knabe in der armen Stube das Spinnrad drehte, hat das große Rad³⁴ geschnurrt, bevor das Zeitalter wieder Mar=morgötter wie diese schaffen konnte."

„Über dies alles sind nun Jahre hingegangen," fuhr der Mond fort³⁵. „Gestern blickte ich auf einen Meerbusen an der östlichen Küste Seelands³⁶ nieder³⁷; da sind herrliche Wälder, hohe Hügel, ein alter Rittersitz mit roten Mauern, in den Grä=ben schwimmen Schwäne, dahinter erscheint zwischen Obstgärten ein Städtchen mit einer Kirche. Viele Kähne, alle mit Fackeln, glitten über die ruhige Fläche, nicht zum Aalfang waren die Feuer angezündet, nein, alles war festlich³⁸. Die Musik er=tönte, ein Lied wurde gesungen, in einem der Kähne stand auf=

recht ber, dem man huldigte, ein hoher, kräftiger Mann, in
einen Mantel gehüllt; er hatte blaue Augen und lange weiße
Haare; ich erkannte ihn und dachte an[39] den Vatikan mit der
Nilgruppe und allen Marmorgöttern, ich dachte an die kleine
5 ärmliche Kammer, wo der kleine Bertel mit dem kurzen Hembe
am Spinnrade saß. Das Rad der Zeit hat sich gedreht,
neue Götter[40] sind aus dem Steine entstanden. — — Von den
Kähnen ertönte ein Hoch[41], **Bertel Thorwaldsen**[42]
hoch!"

Zweiundzwanzigster Abend.

10 „Ich will dir ein Bild aus Frankfurt[1] liefern," sagte der
Mond. „Besonders ein[2] Gebäude betrachtete ich dort, es
war nicht Goethe's[3] Geburtshaus, nicht das alte Rathaus[4],
durch dessen gegitterte Fenster die gehörnten Schädel der Ochsen
noch hervorragen, die bei der Kaiserkrönung[5] gebraten und
15 preisgegeben wurden; nein, es war ein bürgerliches Haus,
grün angestrichen und einfach, nahe an der schmalen Judengasse[6], es war Rothschild's[7] Haus.

Ich blickte durch die geöffnete Thür, die Treppe war hell er-
leuchtet, Bediente mit brennenden Kerzen auf schweren silbernen
20 Leuchtern standen da[8] und neigten sich tief vor der alten Frau,
die auf einem Tragsessel die Treppe[9] hinunter gebracht wurde.
Der Besitzer[10] des Hauses stand mit entblößtem Kopfe und

drückte ehrerbietig einen Kuß auf die Hand der Alten[11]. Es war seine Mutter, sie nickte ihm und den Bedienten freundlich zu[12], und sie führten sie in die enge dunkle Gasse in ein kleines Haus; es war ihre Wohnung; hier hatte sie ihre Kinder geboren, von hier aus war ihr[13] Glück aufgeblüht; wollte[14] sie die verachtete Gasse und das kleine Haus verlassen, so würde das Glück auch sie[15] verlassen! Das war nun ihr Glaube." — Der Mond erzählte weiter nichts; gar zu kurz war sein Besuch heute Abend; ich aber dachte an[16] die alte Frau in der engen, verachteten Gasse; nur e i n Wort, und ihr glänzendes Haus stände[17] an der Themse[18]; nur e i n Wort und ihre Villa läge[19] am Golf von Neapel[20].

„ „Wenn ich das geringe Haus verließe[21], aus dem das Glück meiner Söhne emporblühte, da würde das Glück sie verlassen!" " — Es ist ein Aberglaube; aber von der[22] Art, daß, wenn man die Geschichte kennt und das Bild erblickt, zwei Worte als Unterschrift genügen, um es zu verstehen: „E i n e M u t t e r."

Dreiundzwanzigster Abend.

„Es war gestern in der Morgendämmerung," dieses[1] sind des Mondes Worte, „noch rauchte kein Schornstein in der großen Stadt, und die Schornsteine waren es gerade, die ich betrachtete. In diesem Augenblick kroch aus einem derselben ein kleiner Kopf heraus[2], und dann der halbe Körper, die Arme

ruhten auf dem Rande des Schornsteins. „„Hiob! Hiob²!“ “
Es war ein kleiner Schornsteinfegerjunge, der zum ersten mal
in seinem Leben durch einen Schornstein gekrochen war und den
Kopf darüber herausgesteckt hatte. „„Hiob! Hiob!“ “ Ja, das
5 war freilich etwas anderes, als in den dunklen und engen
Kaminen herumzukriechen! Die Luft wehte so frisch, er konnte
über die ganze Stadt hinweg⁴ nach dem grünen Walde sehen;
die Sonne ging eben auf⁵; rund und groß schien sie⁶ ihm⁷
gerade ins Gesicht, welches von Seligkeit strahlte, wenn es
10 auch⁸ durch Ruß recht hübsch geschwärzt war.

„„Nun kann die ganze Stadt mich sehen!“ “ rief er, „„und
der Mond kann mich sehen und die Sonne auch! Hiob! Hiob!“ “
und dabei schwang er den Besen.“

Vierundzwanzigster Abend.

Gestern¹ Nacht blickte ich auf eine Stadt in China nieder²,“
15 sagte der Mond. „Meine Strahlen beschienen die langen nack=
ten Mauern, welche die Straßen bildeten. Hier und da findet
man wohl eine Thür, sie ist aber verschlossen, denn was kümmert
die Welt draußen den Chinesen? Dichte Jalousieen³ bedeckten
die Fenster hinter den Mauern der Häuser; nur durch die Fen=
20 ster des Tempels schimmerte ein mattes Licht. Ich blickte hin=
ein⁴ und sah die bunte Pracht. Vom Fußboden bis zur Decke
sind mit den grellsten Farben und reicher Vergoldung Bilder

gemalt, die das Wirken der Götter hier auf Erden vorstellen; in jeder Nische stehen Bildsäulen, aber beinahe gänzlich von[5] der bunten Draperie und den herunterhängenden Fahnen versteckt; vor jeder Gottheit, sie sind alle von Zinn, stand ein kleiner Altar mit Weihwasser, Blumen und brennenden Wachs=[5] kerzen; ganz oben[6] aber stand Fo[7], die erste Gottheit, mit einem Kleide von gelber Seide, denn dieses ist dort die heilige Farbe. Am Fuße des Altars saß ein lebendes Wesen, ein junger Geistlicher; er schien zu beten, aber mitten im Gebet in Grübeln zu versinken, und das war sicher eine Sünde, denn seine Wan=[10] gen glühten, und er senkte den Kopf tiefer. Armer Sui=Hong! Träumte er vielleicht, hinter der langen Mauer der Straße, in dem kleinen Blumengarten zu arbeiten, welcher sich vor jedem Hause befindet, und war ihm vielleicht diese Beschäftigung lieber[8] als die, auf die Wachskerzen im Tempel Achtung zu[15] geben? oder gelüstete es ihn, an der reichen Tafel zu sitzen und zwischen jedem Gerichte sich[9] den Mund an Silberpapier zu wischen? oder war seine Sünde gar so groß, daß, wenn er sie auszusprechen wagte, das himmlische Reich[10] sie[11] mit dem Tode[12] bestrafen mußte? Hatten seine Gedanken es[13] gewagt,[20] mit den Schiffen der Barbaren nach ihrer Heimat, nach dem weit entlegenen England zu fliehen? Nein! so weit flogen seine Gedanken nicht, und doch waren sie so sündhaft, wie sie nur[14] von jugendlichem Blute geboren werden können, sündhaft hier in dem Tempel, in Gegenwart Fo's und der andern heiligen[25] Götter. Ich weiß, wo seine Gedanken weilten. Am äußersten Ende der Stadt, auf dem flachen mit Fliesen belegten Dache,

um welches das Geländer von Porzellan gemacht zu sein schien,
wo die schönen Vasen [15] mit den großen weißen Glockenblumen
standen, saß die reizende Pe, mit den kleinen schelmischen Augen,
den vollen Lippen und dem kleinsten Fuße.   Der Schuh war
5 eng, aber noch enger war es ihr [16] um's Herz; sie erhob die
feinen, runden Arme, der Atlas rauschte.   Vor ihr stand eine
Glasschale mit vier Goldfischchen, sie rührte behutsam im Was=
ser herum [17] mit einem bunt bemalten, lackierten Stöckchen, ganz
langsam, denn sie grübelte über etwas; dachte sie vielleicht
10 daran [18], wie reich und golden die Fische gekleidet waren, wie
ruhig sie in ihrer Glasschale lebten, wo sie ihre reichliche Nah=
rung erhielten, und wie viel glücklicher sie doch sein würden,
wenn sie frei herumschwimmen könnten?   Ja, dies begriff die
schöne Pe.   Ihre Gedanken verließen die Heimat, ihre Gedan=
15 ken besuchten den Tempel, aber nicht Gottes wegen [19] weilten
sie dort.   Arme Pe! Armer Sui=Hong!   Ihre [20] irdischen
Gedanken begegneten sich [21], mein kalter Strahl lag aber wie
ein Cherubsschwert zwischen beiden."

Fünfundzwanzigster Abend.

„Es herrschte Windstille," sagte der Mond, „das Wasser war
20 durchsichtig, wie die reinste Luft, durch welche ich schwebte; tief
unter dem Meeresspiegel konnte ich die seltsamen Pflanzen er=
blicken, die wie riesenhafte Bäume des Waldes ihre klafterlangen

Arme gegen mich erhoben; die Fische schwammen über ihre Gipfel hinweg[1]. Hoch in der Luft zog ein Schwarm wilder Schwäne, einer davon[2] sank mit ermatteten Flügeln tiefer und tiefer, seine Augen folgten der luftigen Karawane, die sich mehr und mehr entfernte; weit ausgebreitet hielt er die Flügel und sank, wie die Seifenblase sinkt in der stillen Luft; er berührte die Wasserfläche, sein Kopf bog sich zurück[3] zwischen die Flügel, ruhig lag er da[4], gleich der weißen Lotosblume auf dem stillen Landsee. Und ein leiser Wind erhob sich und kräuselte die leuchtende Meeresfläche, strahlend erschien sie[5], als sei[6] es der Äther, der sich in großen breiten Wogen dahinwälzte; und der Schwan erhob seinen Kopf, und das leuchtende Wasser spritzte wie blaues Feuer über seine Brust und seinen Rücken. Die Morgendämmerung beleuchtete die roten Wolken, der Schwan erhob sich gestärkt und flog gegen die aufgehende Sonne, gegen die bläuliche Küste, wo die Karawane hingezogen war, aber er flog allein, mit Sehnsucht in der Brust, einsam flog er über die blauen schwellenden Wogen."

Sechsundzwanzigster Abend.

„Ich will dir noch[1] ein Bild aus Schweden geben," sagte der Mond. „Zwischen dunklen Tannenwäldern nahe an den melancholischen Ufern des Roxen[2], liegt die alte Klosterkirche Vreta[3]. Meine Strahlen glitten durch das Gitter in das ge=

räumige Gewölbe, wo Könige in großen Steinsärgen ruhig
schlummern. In der Mauer über ihren Gräbern prangt das
Bild der irdischen Herrlichkeit: eine Königskrone, sie⁴ ist aber
nur von Holz, bemalt und vergoldet, und wird durch einen in
5 die Mauer getriebenen Holzstift gehalten. Die Würmer haben
das vergoldete Holz zernagt, die Spinne hat ihr Netz von der
Krone herab⁵ bis auf den Sand gesponnen, es ist eine Trauer=
fahne, vergänglich, wie die Trauer der Sterblichen. Wie ruhig
sie schlummern! Ich erinnere mich ihrer⁶ ganz deutlich. Ich
10 sehe noch das kecke Lächeln um die Lippen, welches so mächtig,
so entscheidend Freude oder Kummer aussprach. Wenn das
Dampfschiff wie eine Zauberschnecke durch⁷ die Berge fährt,
kommt oft ein Fremder nach⁸ der Kirche, besucht das Grabge=
wölbe, fragt nach den Namen⁹ der Könige, und diese klingen
15 tot und vergessen. Er betrachtet lächelnd die wurmstichigen
Kronen, und ist¹⁰ er ein recht frommes Gemüt, so mischt sich
Wehmut in sein Lächeln. Schlummert, ihr Toten! Der
Mond gedenkt eurer¹¹, der Mond senkt in der Nacht seine kalten
Strahlen zu eurem stillen Königreich hinab¹², über dem die
20 Krone von Tannenholz hängt!"

Siebenundzwanzigster Abend.

„Dicht an der Landstraße," sagte der Mond, „liegt eine
Schenke, ihr¹ gegenüber ein großer Wagenschuppen, dessen

Strohdach gerade gedeckt wurde[2]. Ich blickte zwischen den
Sparren hindurch[3] und durch das offene Bodenlager in den un=
wirtlichen Raum hinunter[4]. Der Truthahn schlief auf dem
Balken, der Sattel war in der leeren Krippe zur Ruhe gebracht.
Mitten in dem Schuppen stand ein Reisewagen; die Herrschaft[5]
darin schlief ganz fest, während die Pferde getränkt wurden[6].
Der Kutscher dehnte sich, obwohl er, ich weiß es am besten,
den halben Weg vortrefflich geschlafen hatte. Die Thür nach
der Gesindestube stand auf[7], das Bett sah aus[8], als wäre[9] es
um und um gekehrt, das Licht stand auf dem Fußboden und war
tief in den Leuchter heruntergebrannt. Der Wind strich kalt
durch den Schuppen; es war der Morgendämmerung näher als
der Mitternacht. In dem Sande auf der Erde schlief eine
wandernde Musikantenfamilie; die Mutter und der Vater
träumten gewiß von dem brennenden Naß[10], das noch in der
Flasche übrig geblieben[11], das kleine blasse Mädchen träumte von
dem brennenden Naß ihrer Augen; die Harfe lag bei[12] ihren
Köpfen, der Hund zu ihren Füßen.“

Achtundzwanzigster Abend.

„Es war in einem Provinzialstädtchen,“ sagte der Mond,
„freilich war es im vergangenen Jahre, aber das thut nichts zur
Sache[1], ich sah es sehr deutlich; heute[2] Abend las ich in den
Zeitungen davon, aber da war es lange[3] nicht so deutlich. In

der Gaftftube faß der Bärenführer und aß fein Abendbrot; der
Bär ftand braußen hinter dem Holzftoße angebunden, der arme
Petz⁴, der niemand etwas zu leide that, obwohl er grimmig
genug ausfah. Oben in der Dachkammer fpielten in meinen
5 Strahlen drei kleine Kinder; das ältefte mochte fechs Jahre alt
fein, das jüngfte nicht mehr als zwei. „Klatfch, klatfch!“ kam
es⁵ die Treppe hinauf⁶; wer konnte das wohl⁷ fein? Die
Thür fprang auf⁸ — es war der Petz, der große zottige Bär!
Er hatte Langeweile gehabt unten im Hofe und hatte nun den
10 Weg zur⁹ Treppe hinauf gefunden; ich habe alles gefehen,“
fagte der Mond. „Die Kinder erfchraken fehr über das große
zottige Tier; jedes kroch in feinen Winkel, er entdeckte fie aber
alle drei und befchnüffelte fie, that ihnen aber nichts zu leide.
„„Das ift gewiß ein großer Hund,““ dachten fie, und dann
15 ftreichelten fie ihn; er legte fich auf den Fußboden, der kleinfte
Junge kletterte auf ihn hinauf¹⁰ und fpielte mit feinem goldlocki-
gen Köpfchen Verftecken in dem dichten fchwarzen Pelz. Jetzt
nahm der ältefte Knabe feine Trommel und fchlug darauf¹¹,
daß es dröhnte; der Bär erhob fich auf den Hinterfüßen und
20 fing an¹² zu tanzen; es war allerliebft anzufehen. Jeder
Knabe nahm jetzt fein Gewehr, auch der Bär mußte eins haben,
und er hielt es recht ordentlich feft¹³; es war ein prächtiger
Kamerad, den fie gefunden hatten, und dann marfchierten fie:
„„Eins, zwei, Eins, zwei!““ —

25 Da griff jemand an die Thür, fie¹⁴ ging auf¹⁵, es war die
Mutter der Kinder. Du hätteft¹⁶ fie fehen follen, ihren laut-
lofen Schreck fehen, das kreideweiße Geficht, den halbgeöffneten

Mund, die stieren Augen. Aber der kleinste Junge nickte seelenvergnügt und rief ganz laut in seiner Sprache: „„Wir spielen nur Soldaten!" " — Und dann kam der Bärenführer!"

Neunundzwanzigster Abend.

Der Wind wehte kalt und heftig, die Wolken jagten vorbei[1]; 5 nur ab[2] und zu wurde der Mond auf[3] Augenblicke sichtbar. „Aus dem stillen Luftraum schaute ich hinunter[4] auf die fliegenden Wolken," sagte er, „ich sah die großen Schatten über die Erde hinwegjagen. Ich blickte auf ein Gefängnis. Ein zugemachter Wagen hielt vor der Thür, ein Gefangener sollte[5] 10 darin abgeholt werden. Meine Strahlen drangen durch das Gitterfenster nach[6] der Mauer; der Gefangene ritze zum Ab= schied einige Zeilen darauf, aber es[7] waren keine Worte, die er schrieb, es war eine Melodie, der Erguß seines Herzens. Die Thür wurde geöffnet, er wurde herausgeführt und richtete seine 15 Augen auf[8] meine runde Scheibe; Wolken zogen zwischen uns hin[9], als dürfte[10] er nicht mein Angesicht, ich nicht das seinige sehen. Er stieg in den Wagen, der Schlag wurde zuge= macht, die Peitsche knallte, die Pferde eilten davon[11] in den dichten Wald hinein[12], wohin meine Strahlen ihnen nicht zu 20 folgen vermochten; durch das Gitterfenster aber blickte ich, *meine Strahlen glitten über die in die Mauer geritzte Melodie, sein letztes Lebewohl; wo die Worte fehlen, da sprechen d*

Töne. Nur einzelne Noten vermochten meine Strahlen zu be-
leuchten, der größte Teil wird für mich ewig im Dunkeln
bleiben. War es die Todes-Hymne, welche er schrieb? Waren
es der Freude Jubeltöne? Fuhr er dem Tod entgegen[12] oder
5 der Umarmung seiner Geliebten? Die Strahlen des Mondes
lesen nicht alles, was die Sterblichen schreiben."

Dreißigster Abend.

„Ich liebe die Kinder," sagte der Mond, „namentlich die
ganz kleinen sind so possierlich. Manchmal luge ich zwischen
dem Vorhang und dem Fensterbrett in die Stube, wenn sie
10 nicht an[1] mich denken. Es macht mir Vergnügen zuzusehen[2],
wenn sie sich allein[3] ausziehen müssen. Erst kriecht die kleine,
bloße, runde Schulter aus dem Kleide heraus[4], darauf der Arm,
oder ich sehe, wie der Strumpf ausgezogen wird und ein nied-
liches, weißes festes Beinchen zum Vorschein kommt und ein
15 Füßchen zum Küssen, und ich küsse es!
     Was ich erzählen wollte[5]: Heute Abend blickte ich durch ein
Fenster, vor welches kein Vorhang gezogen war, denn es wohnt
niemand gegenüber[6]. Ich sah eine ganze Schar Kleiner[7], alle
Geschwister, darunter war ein kleines Schwesterchen; sie ist nur
20 vier Jahre alt, kann aber ihr Vater-unser beten, so gut wie ir-
gend einer. Die Mutter sitzt alle Abende an[8] ihrem Bette und
hört sie beten, dann bekommt sie einen Kuß, und die Mutter

bleibt sitzen, bis die Kleine einschläft, und das geschieht so schnell, als sich nur die Äuglein schließen können.

Heute Abend waren die zwei ältesten Kinder etwas ausgelassen; das eine hüpfte auf e i n e m⁹ Beine in seinem langen weißen Nachthembchen, das andere stand auf einem Stuhl, umgeben von¹⁰ den Kleidern aller andern Kinder, es sagte, es wären¹¹ lebende Bilder. Das dritte und das vierte legten die Wäsche fein ordentlich in das Kästchen, und das muß auch gemacht werden; die Mutter aber saß an dem Bette des kleinsten und bedeutete allen, daß sie schweigen sollten, denn die kleine Schwester würde das Vater=unser beten.

Ich blickte über die Lampe hinweg¹² in das Bett der¹³ Kleinen, wo sie auf dem feinen weißen Überzug lag, die Händchen gefaltet und das kleine Gesicht ganz ernsthaft und andächtig; sie betete laut das Vater=unser. „„Aber was ist das?"" unterbrach die Mutter sie mitten im Gebet, „„wenn du gebetet hast: Gieb uns unser täglich Brot! setzest du noch etwas hinzu¹⁴, was ich nicht verstehen kann; du mußt mir sagen, was es ist!"" Die Kleine schwieg und blickte verlegen die Mutter an¹⁵. „„Was sagst du weiter als: Gieb uns unser täglich Brot?"" „„Sei ja¹⁶ nicht böse, liebe Mutter! Ich betete: und recht viel Butter darauf!""

NOTES.

NOTES.

INTRODUCTION.

1. am allerwärmsten und innigsten (lit. warmest and deepest of all.)
2. empfinde, syn. fühle; translate: *when my feelings are warmest and deepest.* **3. so ist mir** = so scheint es mir, *it seems to me.* **4. als wären,** *as if . . . were;* „als" in the sense of „als ob", „als wenn", „wie wenn" is followed by the subjunctive. **5. mir Hände und Zunge** for „meine Hände und Zunge"; a dative grammatically dependent on a verb often takes the place of a possessive pronoun, this being especially common with the dative of the personal pronouns. **6. Gäßchen** (dim. of „Gasse" [gate; comp. Highgate, Kirkgate, etc.]), *lane.* **7. es gebricht mir nicht** = es fehlt mir nicht. **8. gezogen,** supply „war"; the auxiliaries „haben" and „sein" are often omitted in dependent sentences. **9. war es mir** = fühlte ich mich; schien es mir; comp. Note 3. **10. einen** is here numeral = *one,* therefore with emphasis. **11. eines Abends,** *one evening;* the genitive is used to express indefinite time in answer to the question "*when?*" **12.** see hinaus*blicken. **13. er,** (referring of course to „der" Mond) *she* or *it.* **14.** see zu*werfen. **15.** see herein*scheinen. **16. wolle** (present subjunct.). The subjunctive is the mood of an indirect statement, in which the speaker expresses the words or ideas of another in his own words — *that he would . . .* **17. schade** — elliptically for „es ist schade". **18. die vorige Nacht oder denselben Abend.** — The accusative is used to express definite time in answer to the question

53

"when ?" comp. Note 11. **19. male du nur,** *just sketch* (paint)! **20. Tausend und eine Nacht,** "Thousand and One Nights" more commonly called " *The Arabian Nights' Entertainments* ", a book originally written in Arabic and first introduced into Europe by the French orientalist Antoine Galland in 1704. **21. würde doch wohl,** their number would, *I fear*, (*I think*). **22. die** = **diejenigen,** *those,* supply „**Geschichten**", (stories).

---•◦•---

FIRST EVENING.

1. Ganges, the principal river of Hindostan. **2.** English word-order: „**durch das dichte Geflechte der Platanen, gewölbt wie eine Schildkrötenschale**". **3. Hindu-Mädchen,** *a Hindu* (or Hindoo) *girl,* of the native race inhabiting Hindostan. **4.** comp. Milton's " Paradise Lost ", Book IV. 323–324.

> Adam the goodliest man of men since born
> His sons; *the fairest of her daughters Eve.*

5. Lianen, *lianas,* a term applied to the climbing and twining plants of the tropical forests. **6.** see **vorwärts*schreiten. 7.** see **vorüber*springen. 8. in der Hand** = **in ihrer Hand.** — In German the definite article often replaces the possessive adjective when there can be no doubt as to the possessor. **9. sie** (referring to „**die**" **Lampe**), *it.* **10.** see **dahin*gleiten. 11. als wollte sie,** as if it *were* to . . .; regarding the subjunct. impf. **wollte,** comp. Introduction, Note 4. **12.** English word-order: **hinter den langen Seidenfransen der Augenlider. 13. erlosch sie aber,** conditional inversion for: „**wenn sie aber erlosch**". **14.** = **auf ihre Knie;** comp. Note 8. **15. an,** *of;* after the verb „**denken**". **16. Brahma,** in Indian mythology, one of the deities of *the Hindu* trimurti or triad. He is termed the "Creator", while his brothers *Vishnu* and *Siva* are respectively the " Preserver " and the " Destroyer ". 17. see wieber*hallen.

———•••———

SECOND EVENING.

1. **von**, when followed by a passive construction, is *by*. 2. see hin‑unter*bliden. 3. see herum*springen. 4. see aus*breiten. 5. **baran**, *of it;* comp. First Evening, Note 15. 6. **es ist ... her**, *it has been only a few minutes*, or *only a few minutes ago.* — The German present tense is used to express what has been, and still is, especially after „schon" and „seit". 7. see hinein*bliden. 8. see zurüd*schieben. 9. see hinein*schlüpfen. 10. see auf*schreien. 11. see herum*flattern. 12. see hinterher*laufen. 13. = **ihr Vater**; comp. First Evening, Note 8. 14. see zurüd*biegen. 15. **sie um Verzeihung** bitten, *to beg her pardon.* 16. **ihr** bie Augen unb ben Munb for „ihre Augen unb ihren Munb"; comp. Introduction, Note 5.

———•••———

THIRD EVENING.

1. **heute Abend,** to-night; gestern Abend = ? morgen Abend = ? 2. **zu**, *as.* 3. **Logen** (pronounce as in French!) *boxes.* 4. ber **Souffleur'** (pronounce as in French!) *prompter.* 5. „in ber Tonne" would be correct too, the preposition „in" answering here the questions *whither?* as well as *where?* 6. see bei*wohnen. 7. **mit** brinnen sitzen, *to sit in there at the same time.* — Where the compound of „mit" is a substantive, then Mit– usually implies the same as the Eng. fellow–, joint–, con– or sym– in composition, e. g. Mit‑bürger, *fellow-citizen;* where a verb, it may be often rendered by,

along with others; in common with; together with. **8. höher geht über hoch,** *higher excels high.* **9. dem Pöbel wurden die Finger ge= klopft** for „die Finger des Pöbels wurden geklopft" (clubbed). **10.** see bei*wohnen.

FOURTH EVENING.

---

1. see an*fangen. **2.** see nieder*bliden. **3.** The *"Louvre"* in Paris, East of the Tuileries, originally built for a palace and still called one, though it has long ceased to be a state residence. It is occupied as the great national repository of works of art. **4.** see an*gehören. **5.** see umher*bliden. **6. als befände** (subjunct. impf.) sie sich, *as if she were;* comp. Introduction, Note 4. **7.** English word-order: der reiche Samt, besetzt mit goldenen Franfen. **8.** see aus*sehen. **9. Sie kann sagen,** *you can say.* — The usual mode of addressing one or more persons is by the 3rd pers. plu., which is then written with a capital initial letter, thus „Sie können sagen". But the 3rd pers. sing. „Er" and „Sie" were formerly used for addressing a single in- dividual, especially an inferior, in a strongly patronizing tone. **10. ist ge storben,** *died.* **11. für wen hältst du . . .,** *who do you think the old woman was.* The verb „halten" requires the prepos. „für": to hold *for,* take *for.* **12. die Julirevolution,** *revolution of July* (27th—29th, 1830) after which Charles X., king of France 1824–1830, was forced to flee. **13.** viz. July 28th, 1830. **14.** The *"Tuileries"* (lit. brickyards, from "tuile" = tile) on the right bank of the Seine, so called from the tile-works which formerly occupied its site, had con- tinued to be the chief Parisian residence of the French sovereigns, until they were destroyed during the reign of the Commune in 1871. **15. unter** = 1. under; 2. *among.* Here=? **16.** see zusammen*sinken. **17.** *the tricolored flag* or *tricolor,* a flag having three colors arranged in equal stripes. Such a flag was first adopted in France as the national ensign during the first revolution (1789), the colors being blue, white and red, divided vertically. **18. gen** (= gegen), *towards,* is only preserved in phrases like: gen Himmel; gen Often, Weſten, Süden, Norden. **19. die ſilberne Lilie,** *fleur-de-lis* (French = "flower of the lily", corrupted in Eng. to "flower-de-luce") which has long been the distinctive bearing of the kingdom of France. Some coats bear one, others three, others five and some have them spread over the whole escutcheon. **20. Napoléon Bonaparte** (1769–1821) although of humble descent, was emperor of France 1804–1815. **21. die Immortelle,** *immortelle,* a flower commonly called "Everlasting" or "Cudweed", bot: GNAPHALIUM POLYCEPHALUM.

FLEUR-DE-LIS.

FIFTH EVENING.

1. Upsala (Upsal), city and university of Sweden. **2.** see hinunter* öliden. **'3. Fyris** (or Fyrisa) *river,* a small river of Sweden, on which Upsala is situated. **4.** *so-called graves of Odin, Thor and Freya.* — On the large plain extending around Upsala three large barrows (sepulchral mounds) are visible, which by the people are named the graves of Odin, Thor and Freya, three deities of Scandinavian mythology. **5. worauf ... könnte,** *on which he could have it painted.* **6.** see durch*bliden. **7. Methorn,** *mead-horn; drinking horn,* as used by our ancestors and still now, although in a more elaborate form, by the students of the German and Scandinavian universities. **8. ihn** (referring to „der" Namen), *it.* — This refers to the beautiful and accomplished German countess *Amalia von Imhof,* a lady of the court at Weimar, who lived in Upsala from 1804–1810, where she was greatly admired by the Swedish poet *Erik Gustaf Geijer* (1783–1847). **9.** The adverb „ja" has here and in many similar phrases the signification of "*why*". **10. Eleonora d'Este,** sister of duke Alfonso II. of Ferrara, celebrated in many of the finest sonnets of the Ialian poet Torquato Tasso (1544–1595). **11. der Schönheit Rose** — In his "Travels in Sweden" Andersen states: "An old peasant-woman who lives near the supposed grave of Odin hands the tourist the silver-mounted mead-horn, a gift of the Swedish king Karl Johann (1818–1844); the tourist drains the horn in commemoration of the Scandinavian ancestors, in honor of Sweden and to the health of his '*rose*' (= beloved one)."

SIXTH EVENING.

1. „längs des Strandes" would be more in accordance with modern usage, since the prepos. „längs" is more commonly followed by the genitive. **2.** see hin*laufen. **3. ruht am liebsten,** *likes best to rest* (delights in resting) *upon*. **4. ein Hünengrab** (lit. giant's grave), a barrow or sepulchral mound of great antiquity, formed of earth or stones and found in many districts of Europe. **5. wie glaubst du wohl,** *how do you think that* . . . **6. kamen . . . gefahren,** *came driving along.* — After the verb „kommen" the perf. partic. is frequently used in the sense of the pres. partic. to express the manner of motion, e. g. er kommt geflogen, comes flying. **7. das sind,** *these* (those) *are.* — "These" or "those" immediately preceded or followed by the verb "to be" are rendered in German by the neuter pronoun „dies" (or „das"), without any regard to the number or gender of the object pointed at; but the verb will agree with the following *noun.* **8. die Klafter,** *a* cord. — The def. artic. is used in German where English uses the indef. artic., with a distributive sense, e. g. brei Thaler bie Elle, three dollars *a* yard. **9.** fort supply „gefahren" or „gegangen", *gone.* **10.** see bavon*rollen. **11.** see vorüber*fahren. **12.** Paffagie're (pronounce the first three syllables as in French and the final —*e* like —*e* in „Rofe"), *passengers.* **13.** blies ins (= in bas) Horn, *sounded the horn.* — Other instances where a German preposition remains untranslated in English are: „in bie Hände flatfchen", to clap the hands; „mit bem Balle fpielen", to play ball. **14.** ob es wohl, *I wonder whether* ... **15.** benen brinnen, *those inside.* **16.** famen angefprengt; comp. Sixth Evening, Note 6. **17.** hier möchte ich wohl, *here, I think, I should like.* **18.** als fei (subjunct. pres.), comp. Introduction, Note 4. **19.** see vorüber*fahren. **20.** es faßen, *there sat.* — „Es" is made the grammatical subject of a verb, when the logical subject follows later; here = fechs Perfonen faßen barin. **21.** comp. First Evening, Note 15. **22.** fei (subjunct. pres.). — The subjunctive is used in indirect questions; comp. Introduction, Note 16. **23.** bie, here: *these.* — When the def. artic. is used as demonstrat. pron. denoting "this (that) one", it has the accent. **24.** see auf*faffen. **25.** Rossini (1792–1868), a celebrated Italian composer of music; his opera "The Barber of Seville" is the most popular of all his works. **26.** see aus*ruhen. **27.** see ab*legen. **28.** see (fich) hin*biegen. **29.** ihr vor ber Erinnerung for „vor ihrer Erinnerung;" comp. Introduction, Note 5.

SEVENTH EVENING.

1. „Es" hingen fchwere Wolfen for „fchwere Wolfen hingen", *there hung* ... comp. Sixth Evening, Note 20. **2.** see hinaus*fehen. **3.** hätte erfcheinen follen, *should have appeared.* **4.** see umher*fliegen.

5. lit: *What has the moon (he!) not experienced!* **6. die Sündflut** (corrupt. form for Sinflut = "general flood"), *deluge.* **7.** see nieber*=lächeln. **8. Babylon's river,** viz. "Euphrates," which ran through the midst of the town. **9.** with reference to Psalm 137, verses 1 and 2: "*By the river of Babylon we sat down, yea, we wept, when we re-membered Zion. We hanged our harps upon the willows in the midst thereof.*" **10.** referring to Shakespeare's play "Romeo and Juliet". **11. gen Himmel;** comp. Fourth Evening, Note 18. **12.** comp. Introduction, Note 13. **13. der Held auf Sankt Helena** is Napoleon Bonaparte, who after his downfall in 1815 was captured and banished to the island of *St. Helena,* where he died May 5th, 1821. **14.** *What is it that the moon can not relate!* **15. als** (instead of „wie") ich blickte would be more in accordance with modern usage. **16.** see vorüber*ziehen. **17. von,** *by;* comp. Second Evening, Note 1.

EIGHTH EVENING.

1. der Polarvogel, *fulmar,* a swimming bird of the family of the "Petrels"; it is called "PROCELLARIA GLACIALIS" by the scientists. **2. die Lychnis,** a genus of plants, to which our "Evening Lychnis" and our "Corn Cockle" belong. **3. die Nixenblume,** *White water-lily,* bot: NYMPHAEA ALBA. **4. die Nordlichtkrone** ("AURORA BOREALIS"), *the Northern lights,* a luminous meteoric phaenomenon appearing at night and forming an arc with its ends on the horizon. **5. von . . . aus,** *from.* **6. lassen wir nun . . .** for „laßt nun die Seelen . . ." *let the souls of the dead play ball . . .* **7. ihrem Glauben gemäß,** *according to their belief*— the prepos. „gemäß" may *either precede* or follow its case. **8.** see umher*springen. **9.** see auf*treten. **10. Trommel,** here = Maultrommel. **11. waren es,**

elliptic. for „waren davon überzeugt". **12.** nicht nötig **hätte,** *might not need.* **13.** „in **dem** festen Schnee" would be correct too, the prepos. „in" answering here either question *where?* or *whither?* **14.** *Kajak* (or Kayak), a light fishing-boat of the Greenlanders made by fastening seal-skins about a wooden frame. **15.** *Angekok* (sorcerer), *medicine-man* of the Eskimos in Greenland. **16.** see vor*ziehen. **17.** see hinweg*fliegen.

NINTH EVENING.

1. auf einen Hutfilz gesät, *sown upon a piece of hatters' felt.* — " It is a fact, that certain small seeds take root and produce healthy plants by being sown on a piece of old felt, which is put into a dish and kept sufficiently moist." (Simonson). **2. sterbe,** pres. tense for the future: „sterben werde", as often in German, *when I shall die one day.* **3.** werde ich gebracht for „werde ich gebracht werden", *I shall be taken,* comp. Note 2. **4.** see heraus*tragen. **5.** gestorben sei (subjunct.), *had died; was dead.* **6.** see davon*fahren. **7.** see hinaus*rollen. **8. als gelte** (subjunct. pres.), *as if it was for;* comp. Introduction, Note 4. **9.** see durch*gehen. **10. eine Tote** = nach ihrem Tode. **11. über Stock und Stein,** *over hedge and ditch.* — Two words generally synonymous and frequently alliterative or rhyming are often placed side by side in German to make a statement more emphatic, e. g. „mit Mann und Maus, with every soul on board"; „mit Kind und Kegel, with the whole family". **12.** see herab*fliegen. **13.** see auf*steigen. **14. sie sie** (*she it*). — In a case like this, where two words of the same sound come together, the pronoun of the 3rd pers. (sie) as object might better be replaced by „dieselbe, the same". **15.** see (sich) zurück*ziehen.

TENTH EVENING.

1. **Pompeji**, *Pompeii*, an ancient city of Italy, situated near the sea,
15 miles S. E. of Naples.   In the year 79 A. D. it was overwhelmed together with the towns of Herculaneum and Stabiae by an eruption of
Mount Vesuvius, from the crater of which it is distant about 5 miles.   For
more than sixteen centuries its existence appeared to be unknown and

STREET OF THE TOMBS.

its name almost forgotten.   But in 1748, some peasants employed in
cutting a ditch, met with the ruins of Pompeii, which soon became an
object of general interest.   Excavations were commenced in 1755 and
have been continued to the present time.   2. **die Vorstadt** (sub+urbs).
3. **die Straße der Gräber** (*"Street of the Tombs"*) outside of the
"Gate of Herculaneum" in the Northwestern section of the town.—

It was customary with the Romans to place temples, triumphal arches and sepulchral monuments along their principal roads. **4. vor Zeiten,** plu. (lit. times ago), *a long time ago.* **5. Rofen um bie Schläfen** (lit. roses [rose garlands] around their temples). A noun in the accus. („**Rofen**") is sometimes used absolutely with a prepositional or adjective adjunct („um bie **Schläfen**"), to express an accompanying or characterizing circumstance, as if governed by *"with"* or *"having"* understood = *with rose garlands around* or *having roses around* . . . **6. mit ben schönen Schweftern ber Lais,** *with their fair companions;* Lais was a noted Greek woman, who lived at Corinth in the fifth century before Christ. **7. in neapolitanischem Dienfte,** *in Neapolitan service.* — Previous to the union of the Italian states under Victor Emanuel in 1860 the Southern part of Italy together with the island of Sicily formed the kingdom of Naples. **8. eine Schar Frember,** *a troop of travelers.* **9. von jenfeits ber Berge** (= ber Alpen), *from the other side of the Alps.* **10.** see **ein*ziehen. 11. von,** *by;* comp. Second Evening, Note 1. **12. Lavafteine,** *lava blocks;* "lava" being a. rock-matter that flows in a molten state from volcanoes. **13. bie Baffins'** (pronounce as in French!) *basins.* **14.** see **empor*fteigen. 15. ber eherne Hund,** *the brazen dog.* — In the vestibules of the antique Roman houses one could see a dog made of bronze or depicted in the mosaic pavement and underneath the inscription CAVE CANEM! ("Beware of the Dog!") **16. von,** *by.* **17. ber Ausbruch** (out+break, Lat. e+ruptio). **18. ber Tempel ber Benus.** — Near the "Forum Pompeianum" ruins of quite a number of public buildings have been excavated, among which there is a temple of Apollo, generally, but wrongly, called *the temple of Venus.* **19. bie Trauerweibe,** *Weeping Willow,* bot. SALIX BABYLONICA. **20.** bie **Piuie,** "Stone Pine", bot. PINUS PINEA, grows on the shores of the Mediterranean and is often introduced into pictures. **21. unter** = 1. *under. 2. among.* Here =? **22. bas tragifche Theater** —S. E. of the "Forum" are the ruins of the great or *tragic theatre* of Pompeii with accomodations for about 5000 people. **23. vor Jahrtausenden,** *thousands of years ago.* **24.** die **Dekoration** (pronounce **Dekorazion'**), here: *side scenes and background of the stage.* **25. Sorrento** and **Amalfi,** two maritime towns, South of Naples, in a region which is celebrated for the beauty of its scenery. **26. die schmerzerfüllte Mutter.** — In the Roman Catholic Church the Virgin Mary is called "*Our Lady of Dolors*" (Lat.: "Mater dolorosa") on account of her sorrows at the passion of our Lord. **27. vor tausend Jahren,** *thousand years ago.* **28. Glückliche, vom Himmel Begabte** (fem.), *fortunate woman, gifted by Heaven!* **29. fort,** *gone.* **30.** ist v e r g e f f e n u n d v o r ü b e r, pres. tense for the future „wird vergeffen und vorüber fein."

<hr>

ELEVENTH EVENING.

1. der **Redacteur'** (pronounce as in French!) *editor.* **2. felbft,** *himself.* **3. sollten angekündigt werden,** *were to be announced.* **4. der,** *this* (that), *it;* comp. Sixth Evening, Note 23. **5.** say: "*Heavens!*" **6. könnten,** *might.* **7. er ist es,** *it is he.* — Observe the difference between Eng. and German word-order! **8. ja,** comp. Fifth Evening, Note 9. **9. ein wahres Pferd,** *a thorough ass.* **10.** *poor fellow!* **11. fie ist es,** *it is she;* comp. Note 7. **12. Herr Redacteur!** In German, when addressing a person „Herr" or „Frau" must be added to his or her title, e. g. „Herr Profeffor"; „Frau Baronin". **13. will,** *expects.* **14.** das **Genie'** (pronounce as in French!) **15. genial** (pronounce as if pure German!) **16. wäre** = würde sein, *would be.* **17.** see aus*ftechen. **18. es giebt,** *there are.* **19. machen wir,** *let us make,* used as the missing first pers. plu. of the imperative. **20.** see hin*ſchreiben. **21.** ſchreiben kann, *can* write; "can" bearing here something of the meaning of "is liable to". .**22.** der Hiatus (plu. die Hiaten), *hiatus*, in grammar and prosody it means the coming together of two vowels in two successive syllables, e. g. ge–eſſen; alta arbor; deserto in. **23.** der Mäcen' (Lat. Maecenas), name of a celebrated patron of literature at Rome (70–8 B. C.), now proverbially used as a patron and protector of poets; comp. Horatii Flacci Carmina, Lib. I. Ode 1. **24.** ehrlich geſprochen, *candidly speaking*. **25.** davon, viz. „von Ihrem Buche". **26.** laſſen, *to concede; admit.* **27.** (A free translation):

> *How oft unmarked the pearl of genius lies,*
> *While meaner worth is lauded to the skies;*
> *Though this, indeed, be now a story old,*
> *Yet daily still the tale anew is told. —*
>
> (M. MacCormick, Burlington, Vt., Summer School, '91.)

TWELFTH EVENING.

1. The Lüneburg Heath, a barren district of the Prussian province of Hanover, between the towns of Lüneburg and Celle, in the North-western part of Germany. **2.** ſchlug, syn. ſang. **3.** wollten, supply „gehen". — After modal auxiliaries like „wollen, können, dürfen, mögen, ſollen, müſſen, laſſen" the inf. „gehen" and other infinitives of nearly the same meaning as gehen, are frequently omitted. **4.** ihnen das Glück for „wo ihr Glück", comp. Introduction, Note 5. **5.** würde (subjunctive), *would bloom, as they thought* (hoped); comp. Introduction, Note 16. **6.** ſeine Mutter, on account of the grammatical gender of „Mädchen"; ihre Mutter would also be correct. **7.** der abneh= mende Mond, *waning* moon; opp. der zunehmende Mond = ? **8.** an, *of.* **9.** „wie" ein Evangelium, would be more in accordance with modern usage. **10. würde**; comp. Note 5. **11. ja,** *why;* comp. Fifth Evening, Note 9. **12. Kanaan,** *Canaan,* the promised land. **13. dich** (thyself), *yourself.* **14. das breite duftende Blatt,** *broad and fragrant leaf,* representing the exuberant vegetation of the tropical part of America, more especially of Brazil, whither these emigrants were bound. **15.** see **hin*fahren. 16. ja,** comp. Note 11. **17. schienen,** for „erschienen", *appeared.* **18.** viz. die Lüneburger Heide.

THIRTEENTH EVENING.

1. Polichinell, *Punchinello* (or Punch), the chief character in a popular comic exhibition performed mostly by means of puppets, who strangles his child, beats to death Judy, his wife, belabors a police officer, etc. **2. hätte er ...** gehabt, conditional inversion for „wenn er ... gehabt hätte." **3.** er **wäre** geworden = er würde geworden sein, *he would have become.* **4. Columbine,** *Columbine,* is the name of the wife of Harlequin in the popular comic exhibitions. **5. Harlekin,** *Harlequin,* a performer on the stage, masked, dressed in tight parti-colored clothes, covered with spangles. **6.** es **wäre ...** gewesen, *it would have been.* **7.** die **Schön= heit,** *beauty,* as represented by Columbine. **8.** die **Häßlichkeit,** *ugliness* (*beast!*) as represented by Punchinello. **9.** ihm abzuzwingen, *to force from him.* **10. war,** *would be,* to express repeated action. **11.** see fort*fahren. **12.** see hinzu*fügen. **13. ich bin es,** *it is I;* notice the difference between German and Eng. word-order! **14.** viz. *the day when she married Harlequin.* **15. hätte** das Publikum ... **gesehen,** conditional inversion; comp. Note 2. **16. es,** referring to „das" Pub= likum, *they.* **17.** die **Bretter** (boards) for „die Bühne", *stage.* **18. ja;** comp. Fifth Evening, Note 9. **19. bravo!** *well done!* — The word is an Italian adj. and the correct usage is to say "bravo" to a male singer or actor, "brava" to a female, and "bravi" to a company; "*bravissimo*" is superl. = *very well done!* **20. zur Stadt hinaus,** *out of the town.* — Adverbs, like „hinaus", are often used to emphasize the strength of a preposition, e. g. „aus der Erde heraus, out of the ground"; „in den Wald hinein, into the woods". **21.** der **Gottesacker** (lit. God's + acre) = ? **22.** see (sich) nieber*setzen. **23. den Kopf auf die Hände gestützt**; comp. First Evening, Note 8. **24.** see (sich) aus*nehmen. **25. hätte das Publikum gesehen;** comp. Notes 2 and 15. **26. Pulcinella,** Ital. for "Punchinello."

FOURTEENTH EVENING.

1. die Braut (*bride*), in Germany "a lady *betrothed*"; fiancée. **2.** = derjenigen, *to that.* **3.** welches on account of „das Mädchen"; „welche" would be correct too. **4. rufen nach,** to call *for.* **5. von... ab,** *away from;* comp. Thirteenth Evening, Note 20. **6.** see auf*blicken. **7.** was werden wohl, *I wonder what . . .*

FIFTEENTH EVENING.

1. eine andere viz. „Stadt". **2. sie,** referring to „die" Stadt, *it.* **3.** see vor*kommen. **4.** als hörte (subjunct.) ich; comp. Introduction, Note 4. **5.** von ihr, *of it; of the same.* **6.** der **Wittwenschleier** (widow's + veil). **7. der Bräutigam,** opp. die Braut. **8.** das **Mausole'um,** *mausoleum,* a magnificent tomb or stately sepulchral monument, so called from "Mausolus", king of Caria, to whom his widow Artemisia erected a grand monument in 350 B. C. **9.** change the active construction into the passive and translate: *there were never*

heard in its streets. **10.** see herum*schwimmen. **11.** die **Gondel‑**
gondola; comp. Lord Byron "Beppo" st. 19: —

> *Did'st ever see a gondola ? for fear*
> *You should not, I'll describe it you exactly :*
> *'T is a long covered boat that's common here,*
> *Carved at the prow, built lightly but compactly.*
> *Row'd by two rowers, each called "gondolier,"*
> *It glides along the water looking blackly,*
> *Just like a coffin clapt in a canoe,*
> *Where none can make out what you say or do.*

12. das „Forum", *forum*, originally the name of the market-place
in Rome, and also the largest public place in the ancient cities. In
Venice the "Place of St. Mark" is also called by that name. **13.** die
Fliese, *marble flag-stone*, a flat stone used for paving. **14.** der frei‑
stehende hohe Turm, the bell-tower (Ital.: "campanile") of St.
Mark's Church, a lofty and magnificent structure, *stands apart* from the
church, as often in Italy. **15.** see herum*flattern. **16.** von, *by.* **17.**
lehnt sich an, leans *against.* **18.** an, *of.* **19.** die verschwundene
Pracht, *past glory.* — Founded in the year 452 A. D., Venice was for
centuries the "Queen of the Adriatic"; but the golden period of her
commerce passed when the Portuguese Vasco da Gama rounded the
Cape of Good Hope and discovered a new route to the Indies in 1498.
The end of the once famous republic came when in 1797 Gen.
Napoleon Bonaparte took possession of the city during his Italian
campaign. **20.** see herab*hängen. **21.** see aus*ruhen. **22.** das
Joch, *yoke*, a frame to fit the shoulders and neck of a person and sup-
port a pair of buckets or pails, one at each end of the frame. **23.** viz.,
St. Mark's Church; St. Mark being the patron saint of Venice. **24.**
die ehernen Rosse, *the* (four) *bronze horses* over the front-gate of St.
Mark's Church are a work of the Greek sculptor Lysippos (about 350
B. C.). They were first erected at the island of Chios, whence they were

PALACE OF THE DOGES. — BRIDGE OF SIGHS. — STATE PRISON.

taken to Rome under emperor Augustus; in the fourth century after
Christ they were carried to Constantinople, but in the year 1204 were
shipped to Venice, where they remained until transferred to Paris by
Gen. Napoleon Bonaparte in 1797; finally they were returned to Venice
in 1815. **25. das eherne Pferd im Märchen,** *the brazen horse in the
fable.* — Cambuscan, king of Tartary, was presented by the king of
Arabia and India with a *steed of brass*, which, between sunrise and
sunset, would carry its rider to any spot on the earth. All that was re-
quired was to whisper the name of the place into the horse's ear,
mount upon its back, and turn a pin set in its ears. This story is told
by Chaucer in the "Squire's Tale"; Spenser took up the same tale in
his "Fairy Queen", Book IV. **26. die bunte Pracht...,** *the beautifully
painted walls and windows.* **27. es hat das Ansehen** (= es scheint),
als ob..., *it seems as if genius had yielded to the whims of a child.*
28. hätte (subjunct.), after „als ob"; comp. Introduction, Note 4.
29. der geflügelte Löwe, *the winged lion* on St. Mark's Column; the
lion being the emblem of St. Mark, the patron saint of Venice, and in
virtue of this the emblem of Venice also. **30.** see **durch*scheinen. 31.**
der Lazzaro'ne, a name given to the poorer classes at Naples, who
spend most of their time in idling; here the name is applied to the
lowest classes of Venice, though wrongly. **32. die tiefen Brunnen**
(lit. deep wells; Ital.: "pozzi") are called the dungeons under the
Ducal Palace, where once political offenders were kept. **33. die Ge=
fängniffe,** *the State-Prison* or "*Secret Cell*". **34. die Seufzerbrücke,**
the *Bridge-of-Sighs* (Ital.: "Ponte dei Sospiri"), a means of com-
munication between the State-Prison and the palace of the Doges,
where the criminal courts were held. **35. das Tambourin',** *tambourine,*
a musical instrument of the drum-species, to which small bells are
attached. **36. der Bucento'ro,** *Bucéntaur* (from Greek: "βοῦς" =
ox + "κένταυρος" = centaur), originally a mythological monster, half
man and half ox. It was also the name of the superb state-gailey or

state-gondola of Venice, from which the Doge threw a ring into the
Adriatic yearly on Ascension-Day, thus symbolically performing the

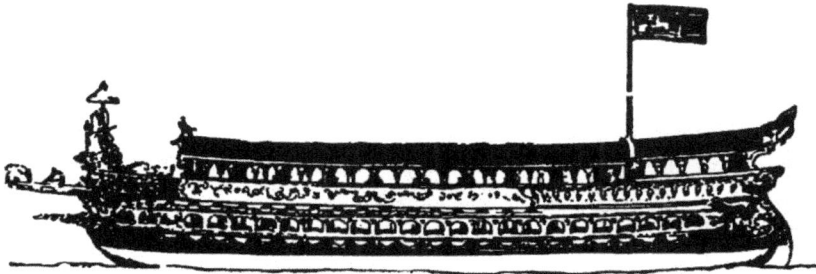

BUCENTAUR.

wedding of the state with the Adriatic; comp. Lord Byron's " Childe
Harold ", IV. 11 : —

> " *The spouseless Adriatic mourns her lord,*
> *An annual marriage now no more renewed;*
> *The Bucentaur lies rotting unrestored,*
> *Neglected garment of her widowhood.*"

SIXTEENTH EVENING.

1. see **herab*ſehen. 2. der Regiſſeur'** (pronounce as in French !)
manager. **3.** see **heraus*treten. 4. mußte er,** supply infinitive
„**gehen**" or „**treten**", *step forward;* comp. Twelfth Evening, Note 3.
5. zum Gelächter werden, *to make one's self the laughing stock.* **6.**
supply „**war**"; comp. Introduction, Note 8. **7.** comp. Eleventh
Evening, Note 7. **8. an,** *of,* after the verb „**denken**". **9. (ſich) aus⸗
nähme** (subjunct. impf.), comp. Sixth Evening, Note 22. **10.** see
empor*blicken. 11. vor einer **Minute,** a minute *ago.* **12. von,** *by;*
comp. Second Evening, Note 1. **13. niemand weiter als,** *no one
else but.*

SEVENTEENTH EVENING.

1. bie **Kaiferburg**, *the Palace of the Caesars*, which once stood on the Palatine, is now a mere mass of ruins. 2. bie **Abler Roma's**, *the eagles of Rome*, because that bird was borne on the Roman standards. 3. **famen — fahen — fiegten**, *came, saw and conquered* — alluding to the laconic despatch, " VENI, VIDI, VICI " ("I came, I saw, I conquered"), which, according to Plutarch, Julius Caesar sent to his friend Amintius in Rome, after he had humbled so quickly Pharnaces, the son of Mithridates, in the battle of Zela, in the year 47 B. C. 4. bie **Peters-firche**, *Cathedral of St. Peter* in Rome, the largest and most beautiful church that has ever been erected. 5. see **hinauf*fteigen**. 6. bas **Kapitäl'**, *capital*, the uppermost part of a column, pillar or pilaster, serving as the head or crowning, and placed immediately over the shaft. 7. see **vorüber*fahren**. 8. see **an*halten**. 9. **woran**, *of what;* comp. also Fourteenth Evening, Note 7. 10. **ihr vom Kopfe** for „von i h r e m Kopfe"; comp. Introduction, Note 5. 11. bie **Marmorfliefe**; comp. Fifteenth Evening, Note 13. 12. see **aus*brechen**. 13. **weinen um**, to weep *for*. 14. see **ba*ftehen**.

EIGHTEENTH EVENING.

1. **es war her**, *it had been.* — The German imperfect tense is used to express what had been, and still was, especially with „fchon" and „feit". 2. **vierzehn Tage** (a fortnight), *two weeks;* but "one week" = a ch t Tage. 3. see **ba*ftehen**. 4. **Fezzan**, *Fezzan*, a kingdom of Northern Africa, bounded by Tripoli on the North, and on all other sides by the Sahara or Great Desert. 5. **ungefäuertes Brot**, *unleavened bread*, such as sea-biscuit. 6. ber **Koran**, *Koran* (or with the article " Al-Koran " =

the book) is the book which contains the religious and moral code of the Mohammedans. It was written by Mohammed. 7. see hin*=zieħen. 8. ein Kind der Sonne, *a child of the Sun.* — The "Tuariks" (or Tuaregs), a people occupying the desert of Sahara westward from Fezzan to the Atlantic, have assumed for themselves the name "Children of the Sun"; they are Caucasian in feature and are very zealous Mohammedans. 9. an, here: *from.* 10. an, here: *of,* after the verb „denken". 11. es war ħer; comp. Note 1. 12. supply „ħatte"; comp. Introduction, Note 8. 13. see ab*feuern. 14. iħr, referring to „die" Karawane. 15. fie, *them.* 16. see ħinweg*zieħen. 17. die Mimosen, *Mimosae* are leguminous shrubs and trees, many of which are remarkable for the irritability of their leaves, and hence they have been termed "sensitive plants". 18. von . . . ħerab, *from;* comp. Thirteenth Evening, Note 20. 19. see zurüď*keħren. 20. an = ?

NINETEENTH EVENING.

1. weinen über, to weep *for.* 2. geschenkt bekommen, *to receive as a present.* 3. es (*it, she*), referring to „das" Mädchen. 4. see mit*=weinen; comp. also Third Evening, Note 7. 5. see ħerab*streďen. 6. see aus*feħen. 7. denen (dat. plu. of the relat. pron.) = welchen. 8. supply „ħat"; comp. Introduction, Note 8. 9. see an*fangen. 10. einbräche (subjunct. impf.) in hypothetical sentences, *would set in.* 11. fie, referring to „die" Puppe. 12. see vor*kommen. 13. als fäħe (subjunct. impf.); comp. Introduction, Note 4. 14. see aus*streďen. 15. ob ich woħl, *I wonder whether;* comp. Fourteenth Evening, Note 7. 16. see nach*denken. 17. see auf*bliďen. 18. see aus*=feħen. 19. mit dem Kopfe schütteln, *to shake one's head;* comp. Sixth Evening, Note 13.

TWENTIETH EVENING.

1. see herab*blicken. 2. der heilige Christoph, *Saint Christopher*
from Greek Χριστὸ + φερω = "one who carries Christ") —
Christopher being of gigantic form, was only to obey the mightiest, as
the legend tells: thus he followed a mighty prince until he found out,
that the same was afraid of the devil: therefore he followed the latter
for some time; soon, however, having discovered that the Evil-one
became frightened by a picture of Christ, he paid homage to Christ as
the mightiest of all. After he had accepted Christianity he was ordered
to carry pilgrims on his shoulders over a river, where there was no
bridge; once he carried a child over, who proved to be the Lord himself, and from that date the name "Christopher" was given him. 3.
der heilige Florian, *Saint Florian*, the martyr (190–230 A. D.), was a
soldier in the Roman army, and was, on account of his being a follower
of Christ, drowned in the river Enns in Austria. He is believed to be a
helper in times of fire. His day is the fourth of August. 4. gleich
(with the dat.) may either follow or precede its case = „g l e i ch einem
Schwalbenneste." 5. see hinaus*fliegen. 6. see vorbei*fahren.

TWENTY-FIRST EVENING.

1. vor mehreren Jahren, "several years *ago*". 2. Kopenhagen,
the capital city of Denmark, where Bertel Thorwaldsen, the greatest
sculptor of modern times, spent his childhood and the last years of his
life. 3. es, *(it)*, on account of the grammatical gender of „das" Kind.
4. sähe (subjunct. impf.). — The subjunctive is used after the verb
„denken" expressing *opinion*, not *certainty;* the subj. pres. „sehe" would
be more in accordance with modern usage. 5. Kuckuck, cuckoo. It

was a " cuckoo-clock ", at the top of which a carved cuckoo appears to announce the hours through as many calls. **6.** baš **Stück** = Stück Möbel, *piece of furniture.* **7. ihm** auf die **Finger** = ſeine Finger: comp. Third Evening, Note 9. **8. wenn er doch ... dürfte** (subj. impf.), *if he only were allowed.* The subj. impf. or pluperf. expresses a wish as unreal or impossible. **9.** see an*ſehen. **10.** see an*ſehen. **11.** see heraus*guden. **12.** see (ſich) um*ſchauen. **13.** see (ſich) hin*ſchleichen. **14.** see an*ſaugen. **15.** see ab*fliegen. **16.** see

LAOCOÖN GROUP.

hervor*ſehen. **17.** Jeſu (Lat. genit.), *in the Lord's name!* **18.** see auf*ſchlagen. **19.** ja, *why.* **20. Bertel** (abbreviat. of „Bartholemäus"), *Bartholemew;* retain the form " Bertel ". **21.** The **Vatican** is the most extensive palace in the world, built upon the Vatican hill, immediately to the North of the basilica of St. Peter's. Since 1378 it has been the principal residence of the popes, and since 1870 their only *residence.* It is also the storehouse of the most valuable literary and *art collections.* **22. Laocoön group,** one of the most beautif

groups of sculpture in the whole history of ancient art. It was discovered at Rome, among the ruins of the Palace of Titus, in 1506, and
was placed in the Vatican by Pope Julius II. ·As the makers of this
group Pliny names the three Rhodian sculptors Agesandros, Polydoros
and Athenodoros (between 300–200 B. C.). — "Laocoön" is a well
known figure from Greek mythology. He was the priest of Neptune
during the Trojan war, who, along with his two sons, was crushed to
death in the folds of two enormous serpents, as represented in the
above mentioned group (comp. Vergil's "Aeneid," book II., verses
200–233.)   **23.** The **"Salon of the Muses,"** one of the large halls

NILE GROUP.

in the Vatican Museum, contains famous statues of the Muses. **24.** see
vor*fommen. **25.** als höben (subj. impf.) fie fich, *as if they heaved.*
26. The **Nile group,** a fine marble statue found during the pontificate
of Leo X. (1513–1521). It was removed to the Vatican by Pope
Clement XIV., and restored by the sculptor Caspar Sibilla. Under
Napoleon I. this statue remained for a while in Paris with its companion-
piece the "Tiber." — "The god Nile, who, on account of the size and
importance of the stream which he represents, could only be rendered
in massive proportions, reclines on his left side with his arm on a
Sphinx, the symbol of Egypt. In the left hand he holds a large
cornucopia filled with flowers and fruit; in his right he holds both fruit

and grain. From the smaller end of the cornucopia waters gush forth and cover all the sides of the base. The stream seems to start from under the garments of the god, as if in allusion to the unknown source of the great river. In the children who are all about, are to be recognized, according to classic authority, the units of measurement of the height of the overflow of the river. This idea is indicated more clearly by. placing the little ones at graduated elevations. Their number, sixteen, is supposed to correspond to the highest measurement to which the overflow reaches. The position and grouping of the children were in a measure necessitated by the manner in which the god reclines upon his four-sided bed. About the empty places to the right and left the children are of course more thickly gathered. On the right, clustering up and down and about the Sphinx and the cornucopia, they seem to lead up to *the little chap who, highest of all, sits in serene complacency with folded arms on the very top of the cornucopia itself.*".. (from *"Bausteine"* by Dr. Karl Friedrichs, Berlin). **27. Sphinx.** — In Egyptian antiquities the Sphinx is a figure having the body of a lion and a human head. There is no historical connection with the Greek fable, in which the Sphinx, a she-monster, proposes a riddle to the Thebans, and kills all who are not able to guess it, finally, when the riddle is solved by Oedipus, slaying herself. **28.** see **ba*liegen. 29.** als **dächte** (subj. impf.) er, *as if he was thinking;* comp. Introduction, Note 4. **30. an,** *of.* **31.** Little Bertel Thorwaldsen was a very pretty child. **32. es waren,** *they were;* comp. Sixth Evening, Note 20. **33.** die **Züge** (plu.) = **Gesichtszüge,** *features.* **34.** = „das große **Rad** der Zeit" (of time). — Remember that the "Nile group" is supposed to have originated about the time of Alexander the Great (336-323 B. C.) **35.** see fort*fahren. **36. Seeland,** *Zealand,* the largest and most important of the islands of Denmark. — The bay referred to is " *Presto Bay* "; the little town near it is *"Nysoe"*, and the nobleman's seat is " *Castle Stampenborg* ", where Thorwaldsen spent the greater part of his last years. **37.** see nieber*bliden. **38.** This scene refers to Thorwaldsen's second return from Rome to Denmark in 1838, when he was received everywhere with the greatest enthusiasm. **39. an,** *of.* **40. neue Götter,** *new gods* — with allusion to some of Thorwaldsen's greatest

BERTEL THORWALDSEN.

creations representing Greek gods, as : Cupid and Psyche; Venus, etc. **41. ein Hoch,** *cheer; hurrah!* **42. Bertel Thorwaldsen** (1770–1844), studied in the Academy of Arts at Copenhagen, and soon after set out *for Rome, where he* remained the greater part of his life. His master-*works are :* The *colossal* statue of Jason, — Triumphal March of

Alexander the Great, — The bas-reliefs "Night" and "Day", — Priam
and Achilles, — Portrait bust of Alexander of Russia, — Monument of
Copernicus, — The wounded and dying Lion, of colossal size, near
Luzerne, Switzerland, etc. . . .

TWENTY-SECOND EVENING.

1. Frankfort-on-the-Main, an old, (formerly) free city of the
Empire, where the old homestead of the Rothschilds is. **2. ein**, here :
one, therefore with emphasis. **3.** Johann Wolfgang Goethe was born
in Frankfort, August 28th, 1749. **4. das Rathaus**, town-hall or senate-
house of Frankfort, called „der Römer". **5.** Up to the year 1531 the
emperors of Germany were crowned at Aix-la-Chapelle, but after that
time the imperial coronation took place at Frankfort. A distinct
feature of the many festivities connected with the coronation was an ox
barbecued, the horned skull of which used to be fastened to the iron-
railed windows of the town-hall. **6. die Judengasse** ("Jews'-Gate").
Previous to the year 1806 the Jews of Frankfort were allowed to live
only in the "Ghetto" or Jews' Quarters of the city, to which the narrow
„Judengasse" belonged. **7. Rothschild's Haus.** — Mayer Anselm
Rothschild (1743–1812), in Frankfort, was the founder of the famous
banking-house. He left five sons, who after their father's death founded
new banking-houses at Vienna, Paris, London, Manchester and Naples,
while their aged mother remained quietly in the old homestead in the
"Ghetto" of Frankfort. **8.** see da*stehen. **9. die Treppe hinunter,**
down stairs. **10. Anselm Mayer Rothschild** (1773–1875), the eldest
son of Mayer Anselm R., was the head of the Frankfort banking-house.
11. die Alte, genit. **der Alten** = „der alten Frau". **12.** see zu*nicken.
13. ihr Glück, *their fortune.* **14. wollte sie,** conditional inversion =

„wenn fie . . . wollte". **15.** fie, *them,* referring to „die Kinder". **16.** an, *of.* **17.** ftände (subj. impf.), *would stand.* **18.** Themfe, *Thames.—* In " London " her third son, Nathan Mayer R., was the chief of a large banking-house. **19.** läge (subj. impf.), *would be situated.* **20.** **Bay of Naples,** a celebrated inlet of the Mediterranean, adjacent to the city of its name, where another son, Karl Mayer R., owned a large banking - establishment. **21.** verliefe (subj. impf.) = „verlaffen würde". **22.** der = „diefer" (or jener), therefore with emphasis.

TWENTY-THIRD EVENING.

1. diefes, *these;* comp. Sixth Evening, Note 7. **2.** aus . . . heraus, *out of;* comp. Thirteenth Evening, Note 20. **3.** Hiob! Hiob! (lit. Job), retain the German form! — To some extent resembling the college cries or yells of our country are the joyous cries of the different trades or corporations of Germany; thus the miners greet each other by: „Glück auf!" ("Good luck!") and the chimney-sweepers by: „Hiob!" **4.** über . . . hinweg, *over;* comp. Thirteenth Evening, Note 20. **5.** see auf*gehen. **6.** fie, *it,* referring to „die" Sonne. **7.** ihm ins Geficht for „in fein Geficht", comp. Introduction, Note 4. **8.** wenn es auch = wenngleich es; obgleich es . . ., *although this.*

TWENTY-FOURTH EVENING.

1. heute Nacht, to-night; geftern Nacht = ? **2.** see nieder*bliden. **3.** die Jaloufie'en (pronounce the first three syllables as in French!) *window-blinds.* **4.** see hinein*bliden. **5.** von, *by.* **6.** ganz oben, *at the very top.* **7. Fo,** *Fo,* the Chinese name for Buddha, the founder of the Indian religion, who died about 540 B. C. **8. lieber,** *more congenial* or: *did he prefer?* **9. fid** den Mund wifdjen for feinen Mund wifdjen, comp. Introduction, Note 4. **10.** das himmlifde Reid, the *Celestial Empire* is China, so called because the first emperors are fabled to have been deities. **11. fie** *(it)* referring to „die" Sünde. **12.** Up to the middle of this century emigration from China was forbidden by penalty of death. **13. es,** idiom., not to be translated! **14. wie ... nur,** *as ever.* **15. Bafen,** *vases* (pronounce B = V in Eng. and not like B in Bater!) **16. ihr um's Herz** for um ihr Herz. **17.** see herum*rühren. **18. daran** *(of it),* idiom., not to be translated! **19.** Gottes wegen; the prepos. „wegen" may either follow or precede its case. **20. ihre,** *their.* **21. fid** (here reciproc.), *one another; each other.*

TWENTY-FIFTH EVENING.

1. see hinweg*fdwimmen. **2. davon,** *of them.* **3.** see (fid) zurüd*= biegen. **4.** see da*liegen. **5. fie,** *it,* referring to „die" Meeresfläde. **6. als fei** (subjunct. pres.)· comp. Introduction, Note 4.

TWENTY-SIXTH EVENING.

1. nod ein, *another,* the first being that of the Fifth Evening. **2.** der Roren, *Lake Roxen,* an inland-lake in the province of East Gotland, S. W. of Stockholm. **3.** die Klofterkirde Breta, the *Conventual Church* (belonging to the cloister) *Vreta,* founded in 1228. Two of its

six chapels contain the remains of Swedish kings. **4. fie,** *it,* referring
to „bie" **Königskrone. 5. von ... herab,** *down from;* comp. Thirteenth
Evening, Note 20. **6. ihrer** (genit. plu.) after „fich erinnern"; *I remember them.* **7. durch,** *along.* **8. nach,** *to.* **9. fragen nach,** *to in-
quire after.* — Among those buried there are Inge II. and his wife
Helena, Valdemar and Magnus Nilsson, all of the dynasty Stenkil. **10.
ift er,** condit. inversion = wenn er . . . ift. **11. gedenkt eurer** (genit.
plu.), *remembers you;* comp. Note 6. **12.** see **hinab*fenken.**

TWENTY-SEVENTH EVENING.

1. ihr gegenüber, *opposite it;* the prepos. „gegenüber" follows its
case. **2. gerade ... wurde,** *was just being.* **3.** see **hindurch*blicken.**
4. in ... hinunter, *down into.* **5. die Herrschaft** (lit. lordship),
gentle-folks, here = traveling party. **6. getränkt wurden,** *were* (being)
given to drink. **7.** see **auf*stehen.** **8.** see **aus*fehen.** **9. als wäre**
(subj. impf.); comp. Introduction, Note 4. **10. das Naß** = 1. fluid,
liquor. 2. humidity, *tears.* **11. geblieben,** supply „war"; comp. Introduction, Note 8. **12. bei ihren Köpfen,** *at their heads,* instead of
the more common „zu ihren Köpfen".

TWENTY-EIGHTH EVENING.

1. thut nichts zur Sache, *is nothing to the point; is irrelevant.* **2.**
gestern Abend, last night; **heute Abend** = ? **3. lange nicht,** *not near.*
4. Petz, the *popular* name of the bear; comp. "Sir Bruin". **5. es**

(it), *somebody.* **6.** see hinauf*kommen. **7. wer ... wohl,** *I wonder who.* **8.** see auf*springen. **9.** = „die Treppe hinauf", *up-stairs.* **10.** see hinauf*klettern. **11.** see darauf*schlagen. **12.** see an*fangen. **13.** see fest*halten. **14. sie,** *it,* referring to „die" Thür. **15.** see auf*gehen. **16. du hätteft sie sehen sollen,** *I wish you had seen her.*

TWENTY-NINTH EVENING.

1. see vorbei*jagen. **2. ab und zu** (off and on), *now and then,* syn. zuweilen; dann und wann. **3. auf,** here: *for.* **4.** see hinunter*schauen. **5. sollte ... werden,** *was to be ...* **6. nach,** *to.* **7. es waren,** *they were;* comp. Sixth Evening, Note 20. **8. auf,** here: *to, towards.* **9.** see hin*ziehen. **10. als** dürfte (subj. impf.); comp. Introduction, Note 20. **11.** see davon*eilen. **12. in ... hinein,** *into;* comp. Thirteenth Evening, Note 20. **13.** see entgegen*fahren.

THIRTIETH EVENING.

1. an, after „denken" = ? **2. zuzusehen,** *to watch them.* — In separable compound verbs (like zu*sehen), the augment ge– of the perf. partic., and also zu when used with the infinitive, are written in one word between the prefix and the verb. **3. allein** (alone), *without assistance.* **4.** see heraus*kriechen. **5. wollte,** *was about to.* **6.** see gegenüber*wohnen. **7. eine ganze Schar Kleiner,** quite a number *of little ones* — a partitive genitive, expressing the whole, of which a *part is taken or a selection made.* **8. an,** here: *near;* by the side.

einem, here: *one*, therefore with emphasis. **10. von,** *by.* **11. es
wären,** *they were* (she said); comp. Introduction, Note 16; comp. also
Sixth Evening, Note 20. — „es feien" would be more in accordance
with modern usage. **12.** see **hinweg*bliden.** **13. der Kleinen** (genit.
sing. of „die Kleine") *of the little girl.* **14.** see **hinzu*feßen.** **15.** see
an*bliden. **16. ja,** with an imperative = *pray!*

VOCABULARY.

VOCABULARY.

A.

a! or **ah!** *oh!*

Aalfang, *m.,* catching of eels.

ab, off. ab und zu, now and then.

Abend, *m.,* evening.

Abendbrot, *n.,* supper.

Abenddämmerung, *f.,* evening twilight.

Abendglocke, *f.,* evening bell.

Abendgruß, *m.,* evening greeting; "good night."

aber, but, however.

Aberglaube(n), *m.,* superstition.

ab/*feuern, to fire off.

ab/*fliegen (flog — geflogen), to fly off, fall from.

Abgabe, *f.,* tax.

Abhang, *m.,* slope, precipice.

ab/*holen, to call for, take away.

ab/*legen, to lay off, put aside.

ab/*nehmen, (nahm — genommen), to wane.

Abschied, *m.,* farewell, departure.

Abschiedsgesang, *m.,* farewell-song.

ab/*schrecken, to frighten.

ab/*sengen, to singe (off), sear.

ab/*zwingen (zwang — gezwungen), to force from.

ach! ah! oh! alas!

acht, eight; eighth.

Achtung, *f.,* attention, heed.

achtungswert, estimable, respectable.

achtzehnt, eighteenth.

Adel, *m.,* noble name, fame.

Adler, *m.,* eagle.

Adria, *f.,* Adriatic (sea).

affektiert', conceited.

ähnlich, similar, resembling. ähnlich sehen, to look like, resemble.

Akt, *m.,* act.

all, all.

allein', alone; but, however.

allerdings', by all means, undoubtedly.

allerliebst', most charming, delightful.

alles, all, everything.

alltäglich, daily; common, ordinary. Alltägliches, everyday happenings, ordinary productions (in literature).

als, as; than; when.

alsdann', then.

alt, old; *comp.,* älter, *superl.,* ältest. die Alte, old woman; die Alten, classics; der Älteste, chief, leader.

Altar, *m.,* altar.

Altertum, *n.,* antiquity.

am = an bem, on the, by the, against the.

Amal'fi, Amalfi.

Ame'rika, America.

A'mor, *m.*, Cupid.

Am'phitheater, *n.*, amphitheatre.

an, on, by, at, against, to.

an'*binden (band — gebunden), to tie on.

an'*bliden, to look at.

an'*brennen (brannte — gebrannt), to light, kindle.

an'*bringen (brachte — gebracht), to get on, fix, construct.

an'dächtig, devout.

An'denken, *n.*, souvenir, relic.

an'der, other; etwas anderes, something different.

an'*fangen (fing — gefangen), to begin, commence.

an'*gehören, to belong.

An'geklagte, *m.*, accused, defendant.

An'gekok, *m.*, sorcer, medicine-man of the Eskimos.

an'genehm, pleasant, agreeable.

An'gesicht, *n.*, face.

ängst'lich, anxious.

an'*halten (hielt — gehalten), to stop.

an'*kündigen, to announce, critisize.

an'*legen, to put on.

an'mutig, pleasant, sweet.

an'*rühren, to touch.

*an'*sehen (sah — gesehen), to look at, gaze at.*

An'sehen, *n*, appearance. das Ansehen haben, to appear, seem.

an'*sprengen, to gallop near.

an'*stimmen, to begin to sing; strike up.

an'*streichen (strich — gestrichen), to paint.

An'strich, *m.*, appearance.

antik, antique.

Ant'litz, *n.*, face.

an'*treten (trat — getreten), to start, set out on.

ant'worten, to answer.

an'wesend, present.

an'*zeigen, to announce.

an'*ziehen (zog — gezogen), to draw tight.

an'*zünden, to light.

A'pfel, *m.*, apple.

applandie'ren, to applaud.

Ara'bien, Arabia.

ar'beiten, to work, be busy.

Ar'che, *f.*, ark.

är'gern, to vex. sich ärgern, to be vexed.

Arm, *m.*, arm.

arm, poor.

Är'mel, *m.*, sleeve.

ärm'lich, poor, shabby, scanty, miserable.

Art, *f.*, kind, sort, fashion.

Ä'ther, *m.*, ether.

At'las, *m.*, silk, satin.

At'lasrod, *m.*, satin gown.

auch, also, too.

auf, on, upon, up, in, for; =geöffnet, open.

auf'*bliden, to look up, gaze up.
auf'*blühen, to bloom forth, rise.
auf'*faffen, to receive, take up.
auf'*führen, to erect; to bring out; to play.
anf'*gehen (ging — gegangen), to open; to rise.
auf'recht, upright, erect.
auf'*richten, to erect.
auf'*fdlagen, to open.
auf'*fdreien (fdrie — gefdrieen), to cry out (in terror).
auf'*fpringen (fprang — gefprungen), to open.
anf'*ftehen (ftand — geftanden), to get up, rise; to stand open.
auf'*fteigen (ftieg — geftiegen), to arise.
auf'*fuchen, to look up, call on.
auf'*treten (trat — getreten), to rise.
Au'ge, n., eye; regard.
Au'genblid, m., moment.
Au'genlid, n., eyelid.
Äug'lein, n., (sweet) little eye.
aus, out of, from. von — aus, from.
aus'*brechen (brach — gebrochen), to break out. in Thränen aus= brechen, to burst into tears.
aus'*breiten, to stretch, spread.
Aus'bruch, m., eruption.
auseinan'der, asunder, apart.
aus'*fallen (fiel — gefallen), to turn out, prove.
aus'*fliegen (flog — geflogen), to start flying.

aus'*gehen (ging — gegangen), to go out.
aus'gelaffen, wild, unrestrained.
aus'geprägt, defined, chiselled.
aus'*heben (hob — gehoben), to unhinge.
aus'*lachen, to laugh at.
aus'*löfdjen, to extinguish.
(fich) aus'*nehmen (nahm — genommen), to look, yield a prospect.
aus'*pfeifen, to hiss (off the stage).
aus'*putzen, to trim up, dress out.
aus'*ruhen, to rest, repose.
aus'*fehen (fah — gefehen), to appear, look.
Aus'ficht, f., view.
aus'*fpannen, to stretch; fich aus= fpannen, to be stretched.
aus'*fprechen (fprach — gefprochen), to utter, express.
aus'*ftatten, to get up, make.
aus'*ftechen (ftach — geftochen), to get the better of, cut out.
aus'*ftellen, to exhibit.
aus'*ftreden, to stretch out.
aus'*wandern, to emigrate.
(fich) aus'*weinen, to weep one's self out, have a good cry.
au'fter, out of, without, outside of.
äu'ftern, to remark.
äu'fterft, remotest.
aus'*ziehen (zog — gezogen), to undress; fich ausziehen, to undress one's self.

B.

Ba'bylon, Babylon.

Bajonett', n., bayonet.

Bajonett'ftich, m., bayonet-thrust.

balb, soon.

Bal'ken, m., beam, rafter.

Balkon' (French!), m., balcony.

Ball, m., ball.

bang(e), anxious, frightened. dem kleinen Mädchen war bange, the little girl felt frightened.

Bank, f., bench.

Bär, m., bear.

Barbar', m., barbarian (plu. die Barbaren = the English).

Bä'renführer, m., bear-leader, owner of a (trained) bear.

Bart, m., beard.

Baffin' (French!), n., basin.

bau'en, to build, form.

Bau'er, m., peasant.

Bau'ernfamilie, f., peasant-family.

Baum, m., tree.

be'ben, to tremble.

Be'cken, n., basin.

bede'cken, to cover.

bedeu'ten, to mean; to signify; give to understand.

Bedien'te, m., (male) servant, menial.

befe'ftigen, to fasten, tie.

(fich) befin'den (befand — befun=
ben), to be found, be.

begabt', gifted.

(fich) begeg'nen, to meet (one another).

bege'hen (beging — begangen), to commit.

begei'ftern, to inspire.

Begei'fterung, f., inspiration, enthusiasm.

begin'nen (begann — begonnen) to begin, commence.

beglei'ten, to accompany, escort.

Beglei'ter, m., escort, follower of a funeral, mourner.

begra'ben (begrub — begraben), to bury.

Begräb'nis, n., funeral; = Grab, tomb.

Begräb'nistag, m., day of burial.

begrei'fen (begriff — begriffen), to comprehend, understand.

begrü'ßen, to greet.

behut'fam, careful, cautious.

bei, at, on, with, together with.

bei'be, both.

Bei'fall, m., applause.

Bein, n., leg.

beina'he, almost.

Bein'chen, n., little leg.

bei'*wohnen, to be present.

bekannt', known, familiar.

beklei'den, to dress, cover.

bekom'men (bekam — bekommen), to get, receive.

bela'ben (belub — belaben), to load.

Belei'bigte, m., offended one, plaintiff.

bele'gen, to cover.

bele'fen, well read, informed.

beleuch'ten, to light up, illumine.

Beleuchtung, *f.*, light, illumination.
bemalen, to paint (over).
bemerken, to remark.
beobachten, to watch.
berechnen, to calculate.
bereits', already.
Berg, *m.*, mountain.
Bertel (*abbrev.* = Bartholemäus), Bertel.
berühren, to touch.
Beschäftigung, *f.*, occupation, work.
bescheinen (beschien — beschienen), to shine upon.
beschnüffeln, to snuffle, smell at.
Beschützer, *m.*, patron.
Besen, *m.*, broom.
besetzen, to trim.
besitzen (besaß — besessen), to possess, own.
Besitzer, *m.*, possessor, owner.
besonders, especially.
besprechen (besprach — besprochen), to criticize.
besser, better.
best, best; am besten, very well.
besteigen (bestieg — bestiegen), to ascend, mount.
bestimmen, to intend, destine.
bestimmt', certain, definite.
bestrafen, to punish, fine.
bestrahlen, to shine upon, beam upon.
Besuch', *m.*, visit, call.
besuchen, to visit, call on.
Besuchende, *m.*, visitor, traveler, *excursionist.*
beten, to pray.

betrachten, to watch, gaze at, survey.
betreten (betrat — betreten), to enter, set foot on.
betrübt', sad, afflicted, melancholy.
Bett, *n.*, bed.
Bettvorhang, *m.*, bed-curtain.
bevor', before.
bewachen, to watch.
bewachsen (bewuchs — bewachsen), to grow over.
bewegen, to move, stir; sich bewegen, to move, stir one's self.
bewegt', excited, agitated; lively.
Bewegung, *f.*, motion.
beweinen, to bewail, weep over.
bewillkommnen, to welcome, greet.
bezahlen, to pay.
Bild, *n.*, picture.
bilden, to form.
Bilderbuch, *n.*, picture-book.
Bildsäule, *f.*, statue.
(ich) **bin,** (I) am.
binden (band — gebunden), to tie, bind.
Bindfaden, *m.*, string.
bis, to; till, until.
(du) **bist,** (thou) art, you are.
bitten (bat — gebeten), to ask, beg.
bitter, bitter.
bitterlich, bitterly, convulsively.
blankpoliert, brightly polished, shining.
blasen (blies — geblasen), to blow; play (on).
blaß, pale.
Blatt, *n.*, leaf, foliage.
blau, blue.

blau′grau, bluish-gray.

bläu′lich, bluish.

blei′ben (bieb — geblieben), to stay, remain.

bleich, pale, pallid.

Blei′gewicht, *n.*, leaden weight.

Blick, *m.*, glance, look.

bli′cken, to look at, gaze at.

Block, *m.*, block.

blond, flaxen-haired.

bloß, bare, naked.

blü′hen, to bloom.

Blu′me, *f.*, flower.

Blu′mengarten, *m.*, flower-garden.

Blu′menkranz, *m.*, wreath, chaplet of flowers.

Blut, *n.*, blood.

blu′ten, to bleed; blutend, bleeding.

blu′tig, bloody.

blu′tigrot, blood red.

Bo′denlager, *n.*, garret.

Bo′gen, *m.*, arch; bow.

Bo′gengang, *m.*, arcade.

bös (böse), naughty; angry. das Böse, the evil.

Bos′heit, *f.*, wickedness.

Bra′ma (Brahma), Brama (Brahma).

bra′ten, to roast.

braun, brown, sunburnt.

Braut, *f.*, bride, affiancée.

Braut′anzug, *m.*, bridal dress.

Bräu′tigam, *m.*, bridegroom.

Braut′ring, *m.*, bridal ring.

Braut′staat, *m.*, bridal attire, bridal dress.

bre′chen (brach — gebrochen), to break.

breit, broad, wide; lengthy.

brei′ten, to spread.

bren′nen (brannte — gebrannt), to burn, glow; brennend, burning, lighted.

Brenn′holz, *n.*, fire-wood.

Brenn′nessel, *f.*, (burning) nettle.

Brett, *n.*, board; *plu.*, die Bretter, (boards), stage, theatre.

brin′gen (brachte — gebracht), to bring, furnish.

Brom′beerranke, *f.*, blackbeery-vine, bramble-bush.

Brot, *n.*, bread.

Bruch′stück, *n.*, fragment.

Bru′der, *m.*, brother.

Brun′nen, *m.*, well.

Brust, *f.*, breast, chest; heart, mind.

Bucento′ro, *m.*, Bucentaur.

Buch, *n.*, book.

Bu′che, *f.*, beech.

Buch′stabe, *m.*, letter of the alphabet.

Büh′ne, *f.*, stage.

bunt, bright, gay-colored.

bunt′farbig, gay-colored.

bür′gerlich, of a citizen, private.

Bür′germeister, *m.*, mayor.

Bür′germeisterin, *f.*, the mayor's wife.

Bür′gersleute, *plu.*, citizens.

Bur′sche, *m.*, fellow.

Busch, *m.*, bush.

Bu′sen, *m.*, bosom.

But′ter, *f.*, butter.

C.

Champag′ner, *m.,* champagne (-wine).

Cha′os, *n.,* chaos, confusion.

Che′rub, *m.,* Cherub.

Che′rubsschwert, *n.,* sword of a Cherub.

Chi′na, China.

Chine′se, *m.,* Chinese.

Chor, *m.,* chorus.

Christi′ne, Christina; **des Müllers Christine,** Christina, the miller's daughter.

Christkind, *n.,* infant Christ.

Chri′stoph, Christopher.

Chri′stus, Christ.

Columbi′ne, *f.,* Columbine.

Coulis′se, *f.,* side-scene.

Cypres′se, *f.,* cypress.

D.

da, there; then.

da′bei, by it, by them; at the same time.

Dach, *n.,* roof.

Dachkammer, *f.,* garret-room.

da′durch, by that.

dage′gen, on the contrary.

daheim′, at home.

dahin′*gleiten (glitt — geglitten), to glide along.

dahin′*rollen, to roll along.

dahin′ter, behind it (them).

(sich) dahin′*wälzen, to roll along.

da′*liegen (lag — gelegen), to lie there.

da′mals, then, in those days.

Da′me, *f.,* lady.

damit′, that.

Däm′merung, *f.,* twilight.

Dampf′boot, *n.,* steam-boat.

Dampf′schiff, *n.,* steam-ship.

dane′ben, near it, by it.

dann, then.

dan′nen, there; **von dannen,** thence, away.

dar′an, (on it), of it (them).

dar′auf, on it (them); thereupon, afterward.

darauf′*schlagen (schlug — geschlagen), to beat on (it).

(sich) darauf′*setzen, to seat one's self on.

dar′aus, of it, out of it; without.

dar′*bringen (brachte — gebracht), to offer.

darein′, into it (them).

darin′, in it (them); inside, within.

darü′ber, over it (them).

dar′um, therefore.

darun′ter, under it (them); among them.

da′*stehen (stand — gestanden), to stand there.

daß, that, so that.

da′von, of it (them); away from it (them); thence.

davon′*eilen, to hurry away.

davon′*fahren (fuhr — gefahren), to drive away.

davon′*laufen (lief — gelaufen), to run away.

davon′*rollen, to roll (ride) along.

da'zu, to it; for it, at the same time.

dazwi'ſchen, there between, between them; at intervals.

debütie'ren (French!), to make one's debut.

De'cke, f., cover, blanket; ceiling.

de'cken, to cover.

deh'nen, to stretch; ſich dehnen, to stretch one's self.

dein, deine, dein, (thy, thine), your.

Dekoration', f., scenery.

de'nen, (dat. plu.) them, to them, for them; in denen, in which.

den'ken (dachte — gedacht), to think.

Denk'mal, n., monument.

Denk'ſtein, m., monument.

denn, for.

den'noch, yet.

der, die, das, the.

de'ren, (gen. sing. fem. and plu.), its, whose; of which.

de'rer, its, of them.

der'jenige, diejenige, dasjenige, that one; diejenigen, those.

derſel'be, dieſelbe, daſſelbe, the same.

des'halb, on account of it, therefore.

deſ'ſen, of which, whose.

deut'lich, clear, distinct.

deutſch, German.

Deutſch'land, Germany.

dich, (thee), you.

dicht, thick, dense; adv., close (by).

Dich'ter, m., poet.

Dich'terkrone, f., poet's crown, laurel.

Dick'icht, n., thicket, bushes.

die'nen, to serve.

Dienſt, m., service.

dies, this.

die'ſer, dieſe, dieſes, this.

dir, (thee, to thee), you, to you.

Direk'tor, m., manager.

Di'ſtel, f., thistle.

doch, yet, after all.

don'nern, to thunder.

dop'pelt, double.

Dorn, m., thorn.

dor'nig, thorny, prickly.

dort, there.

dort'hin, thither, there.

drän'gen, to press; gedrängt voll, crowded.

Draperie', f., drapery.

drau'ßen, outside; without.

dre'hen, to turn; ſich drehen, to turn, revolve.

drei, three.

drei'farbig, tricolored.

drei'zehnt, thirteenth.

drei'ßigſt, thirtieth.

drin'gen (drang — gedrungen), to press, pierce.

drin'nen, inside, within.

dritt, third.

dro'hen, to threaten.

dröh'nen, (to drone). to resound, shake.

drol'lig, droll, odd.

drü'cken, to press.

du, (thou), you.

Duft, m., fragrance.

duf'ten, to emit fragrance; duftend, fragrant.

dun'kel, dark; das Dunkel, darkness.

dun'kelbraun, darkbrown.

durch, through.

durchaus', (throughout), at all; durchaus nicht, not at all.

durch'*blicken, to look through.

durch'*gehen (ging — gegangen), to run away.

durch'*hecheln, (to hackle thoroughly), to critizise severely.

durch'*scheinen (schien — geschienen), to shine through.

durch'sichtig, clear, transparent.

durchströ'men, to permeate.

dür'fen, (pres, ich darf — impf., durfte — p. p., gedurft), to dare, be allowed.

dürf'tig, poor, scanty.

Durft, m., thirst.

E.

e'ben, even; just.

E'bene, f., plain.

e'benfalls, likewise.

echt, genuine.

E'cke, f., corner.

e'he, before.

e'hern, of brass, brazen.

ehr'erbietig, respectful, reverential.

ehr'lich, honest.

Ei'che, f., oak.

Ei'dechse, f., lizard.

ei'gen, own.

eigentüm'lich, strange.

ei'len, to hasten, hurry.

Eil'wagen, m., stage-coach.

Ei'mer, m., bucket, pail.

ein, eine, ein, a, one.

einan'der, one another, each other.

ein'*brechen (brach — gebrochen), to set in.

ei'ner, one.

ein'fach, simple, plain.

Ein'gang, m., entrance.

ein'geladen, invited; der Eingeladene, guest.

ein'*hauen (hieb — gehauen), to cut into, engrave.

ei'nige, some, several.

ein'mal, once, sometime.

eins, one, = das eine, one.

ein'sam, lonesome.

Ein'samkeit, f., solitude.

ein'*schlafen (schlief — geschlafen), to fall asleep.

ein'*schlagen (schlug — geschlagen), to demolish, smash.

ein'*schneiden (schnitt — geschnitten), to cut into.

einst, once, formerly.

ein'zeln, single.

ein'*ziehen (zog — gezogen), to enter.

ein'zig, only.

Eis, n., ice.

Eis'bär, m., polar-bear.

Eis'bär=Ball, m., dance of polar-bears.

eis'bedeckt, ice-covered.

Eis'berg, m., iceberg.

ei'sern, iron, of iron.

Eis'fläche, f., ice-field.

Eis'scholle, f., cake of ice.

Elasticität', f., elasticity.

Elefant', m., elephant.

e'lend, miserable, pitiful, wretched.

Eleono're, Eleanor.

elf, eleven.

elft, eleventh,

Elle, f., (ell), yard.

el'lenhoch, (ell-high), a yard high.

el'lenlang, (ell-long), a yard long.

empfeh'len (empfahl — empfohlen), to recommend.

empfin'den (empfand — empfun= den), to feel.

empor', up.

empor'*blicken, to look up, gaze up.

empor'*blühen, to rise, drive up.

empor'*schießen (schoß — geschof= fen), to shoot up, spring up.

empor'*steigen (stieg — gestiegen), to rise.

Ende, n., end.

eng(e), narrow, oppressed, sad.

Eng'land, England.

En'kel, m., grandson.

Enkelin, f., granddaughter.

entblö'ßen, to bare, uncover.

entde'cken, to discover.

En'te, f., duck.

(sich) entfer'nen, to leave, with-draw.

entfernt', distant, away.

entge'gen, toward, against.

entge'gen*fahren (fuhr — gefah= ren), to drive away to meet.

entle'gen, far-off.

entschei'dend, firmly, decidedly.

entschwin'den (entschwand — ent= schwunden), to vanish, disappear.

entste'hen (entstand — entstanden), to spring, take rise.

er, he.

erbärm'lich, miserable, wretched.

erbli'cken, to see, perceive.

Er'de, f., earth, ground; der Erden, old dat.

erfah'ren (erfuhr — erfahren), to learn, hear.

erfin'den (erfand — erfunden), to invent.

erfül'len, to fill.

Erguß', m., effusion.

erha'ben, lofty, sublime. das Er= habene, sublime.

erhal'ten (erhielt — erhalten), to receive.

(sich) erhän'gen, to hang one's self.

erhe'ben (erhob — erhoben), to raise; sich erheben, to arise.

(sich) erin'nern, to remember.

Erin'nerung, f., remembrance, memory.

erken'nen (erkannte — erkannt), to recognize.

Er'kerfenster, n., bow-window.

erklim'men (erklomm — erklom= men), to climb (up).

erklin'gen (erklang — erklungen), to sound ring.

erle'ben, to experience.

erleuch'ten, to light, illuminate.

erlö'schen (erlosch — erloschen), to extinguish.

ermat'ten, to grow tired.

ernst, earnest, grave.

ernſt'haft, earnest, grave.
erre'gen, to excite.
errei'chen, to reach.
errich'ten, to errect.
erſchal'len, to sound, ring.
erſchei'nen (erſchien — erſchienen),
  to appear, seem.
Erſchei'nung, f., appearance; eine
  ſo luftige Erſcheinung, she was of
  so airy appearance.
erſchre'cken (erſchrak · — erſchrocken),
  to be frightened.
erſchro'cken, frightened, from fright.
erſchwin'gen (erſchwang — er=
  ſchwungen), to raise, afford.
erſt, first.
erſte'hen (erſtand — erſtanden), to
  rise.
(ſich) erſtre'cken, to extend.
ertö'nen, to sound.
erwa'chen, to awake.
erwach'ſen (erwuchs — erwachſen),
  to grow up.
erwar'ten, to expect.
erwi'dern, to answer, reply.
erzäh'len, to tell, relate.
es, it; so.
E'ſel, m., ass.
eſ'ſen (aß — gegeſſen), to eat.
E'ſte, Este (ducal family).
et'was, something; ſo etwas, such
  a thing.
eu'er (eurer), (of you), you.
Euro'pa, Europe.
E'va, Eve.
Evange'lium, n., gospel.
e'wig, everlasting.

F.

Fa'ckel, f., torch, torch-bearer.
Fah'ne, f., flag.
fah'ren (fuhr — gefahren), to drive,
  ride.
Fah'rende, m., one who drives
  (drove) by.
Fahr'weg, m., carriage-road.
Fall, m., fall.
fal'len (fiel — gefallen), to fall.
fäl'len, to give, pass.
falſch, false.
fal'ten, to fold; ſich falten, to be
  folded.
Fami'lie, f., family,
Fami'lienbegräbnis, n., family-
  vault.
Fang, m., catching, hunting.
Far'be, f., color.
faſ'ſen, to catch, seize.
Fe'enſchloß, n., fairy-palace.
feh'len, to ail, need.
Feh'ler, m., fault, defect.
fei'ern, to celebrate.
Fei'genbaum, m., fig-tree.
fein, fine, delicate, very pretty.
feind'lich, hostile.
Feld, n., field.
Fell, n., skin, hide.
Fels, m., rock.
Fel'ſen, m., rock.
Fel'ſenblock, m., block of a rock.
Fel'ſenwand, f., rocky-wall.
Fen'ſter, n., window.
Fen'ſterbrett, n., window-sill.
Fen'ſterloch, n., window-hole.

fern, far, distant.

fer'ner, further, longer, more.

fest, firm, hard, sound.

fest'*halten (hielt — gehalten), to hold fast.

fest'lich, festive.

Fe'stung, f., fort, fortress.

Feu'er, n., fire.

Feu'erfäule, f., pillar of fire.

Fez'zan, Fezzan (country).

Fich'te, f., fir-tree, pine.

Fie'ber, n., fever.

Figur', f., figure.

fin'den (fand — gefunden), to find.

Fin'ger, m., finger.

fin'ster, dark, gloomy.

Fisch, m., fish.

flach, flat.

Flä'che, f., even surface, plain.

fla'ckern, to flicker.

Flag'ge, f., flag.

Flam'me, f., flame.

flam'men, to flame, flicker.

Fla'sche, f., flask, bottle.

flat'tern, to flutter.

flech'ten (flocht — geflochten), to braid.

Fleisch, n., flesh.

flie'gen (flog — geflogen), to fly.

flie'hen (floh — geflohen), to flee, escape.

Flie'se, f., flag-stone.

flie'ßen (floß — geflossen), to flow.

flink, nimble, agile, alert.

Flor, m., growth, bloom; crape.

Flo'rian, Saint-Florian.

flüch'tig, hasty; fleeting; **flüchtige Umrisse,** mere outlines.

Flug, m., flight, speed.

Flü'gel, m., wing.

Flug'sand, m., quicksand.

Fluß, m., river.

Fluß'gott, m., river-god.

Flut, f., flood.

Fo, Fo (Chinese deity).

fol'gen, to follow.

Form, f., form.

fort'*brennen (brannte — gebrannt), to continue burning.

fort'*fahren (fuhr — gefahren), to continue, go on.

Fo'rum, n., Forum.

fra'gen, to ask.

Frank'furt, Frankfort-on-the-Main.

Frank'reich, France.

Fran'se, f., fringe.

Frau, f., woman, wife.

frei, free.

frei'lich, surely, indeed.

frei'stehend, standing apart, isolated.

Frem'de, m., stranger; **ein Fremder,** a stranger, traveler.

Freu'de, f., joy.

Freudenschuß, m., firing of the guns in token of joy.

freu'dig, joyful.

(sich) freu'en, to rejoice, enjoy.

Freund, m., friend.

Freun'din, f., (lady) friend.

freund'lich, friendly.

Frey'a, Freya.

frisch, fresh, cool; newly.

fromm, pious, feeling.

früh, early, soon.

früher, formerly, in former times, prior, sooner.

Frühjahr, n., spring.

Fuder, n., cart-load.

fühlen, to feel.

führen, to lead, carry.

füllen, to fill.

Füllhorn, n., horn of plenty, cornucopia.

fünf, five.

fünft, fifth.

fünfzehnt, fifteenth.

funkeln, to sparkle; funkelnd, sparkling.

für, for.

fürchten, to fear.

Fürst, m., prince.

Fürstenpaar, n., princely couple.

Fuß, m., foot.

Fußboden, m., floor.

Füßchen, n., little foot.

Fyris, m., Fyris (river).

G.

Gabe, f., gift, addition.

Gang, m., walk.

Ganges, m., Ganges (river).

ganz, whole, entire; das Ganze, the whole affair.

gänzlich, wholly, entirely.

gar, very, indeed, too; gar zu, altogether too; gar nicht, not at all.

Garten, m., garden.

Gasse, f., narrow street, lane.

Gäßchen, n., lane.

Gast, m., guest.

Gaststube, f., room for guests, strangers' room.

Gazelle, f., gazelle.

gebären (gebar — geboren), to give birth, bring forth.

Gebäude, n., building.

geben (gab — gegeben), to give, yield; es giebt, there is (are).

Gebet, n., prayer.

geblümt, flowered, sprigged.

gebrechen (gebrach — gebrochen), to be wanting.

Geburtshaus, n., house of one's birth.

Gebüsch, n., bushes, thicket.

Gedächtnis, n., memory.

Gedanke(n), m., thought.

gedankenvoll, thoughtful.

gedenken (gedachte — gedacht), to remember.

gedrängt, thronged; gedrängt voll, crowded.

gefahrlos, without danger, safe.

gefallen (gefiel—gefallen), to please.

Gefangene, m., prisoner; ein Gefangener, a prisoner.

Gefängnis, n., prison.

Gefäß, n., vessel.

Geflecht, n., texture, twist; twisted branches.

geflügelt, winged.

Gefühl, n., feeling.

gegen, toward; against.

gegenüber, opposite.

gegenüber*wohnen, to live on the opposite side (of the street).

Ge'genwart, f., presence.
gegit'tert, iron-railed.
Geg'ner, m., opponent, adversary.
Geheim'nis, n., secret, mystery.
ge'hen (ging — gegangen), to go;
es ging noch schneller, the coachman drove still faster.
gehörnt', horned.
Geist, m., ghost.
Gei'stige, n., intellect, mind.
Geist'liche, m., clergyman, priest.
Geläch'ter, n., laughter; laughing.
Gelän'der, n., railings, balustrade.
gelan'gen, to reach, be admitted.
gelb, yellow.
Geld, n., money.
Gelieb'te, m. and f., beloved one;
lover — sweetheart.
gel'ten (galt — gegolten), to be
for; to mean.
gelü'sten, to long for.
Gemach', n., apartment, room.
Gemah'lin, f., consort, spouse;
wife, bride.
Gemäl'de, n., picture.
gemäß', according to.
gemau'ert, of stone.
Gemein'platz, m., commonplace.
Gemüt', n., soul, heart.
gen, toward.
genau', precise, exact.
genial', of genius, ingenious; odd,
queer.
Genie', n. (French!), genius.
genug', enough, plenty of.
genü'gen, to suffice.
gera'de, straight; just.

geräu'mig, spacious.
Gericht', n., court; dish, mess.
„Gericht und Urteil", court and
judgment (a play).
gering', low, mean, cheap, plain.
gern, gladly.
Geruch', m., fragrance.
Gesang', m., song, hymn.
Gesang'buch, n., hymn-book.
geschäf'tig, busy.
gesche'hen (geschah — geschehen),
to occur, happen.
Geschich'te, f., history, story.
Geschlecht', n., generation; das
neue Geschlecht, present generation.
Geschwi'ster, (plu.), brothers and
sisters.
Gesell'schaft, f., company.
Gesicht', n., face.
Gesin'destube, f., servants' room.
Gespenst', n., spectre.
gespen'sterhaft, spectre-like, ghost-
like.
gespen'stig, spectral, ghost-like.
Gestalt', f., form, figure.
ge'stern, yesterday.
Gesträuch', n., shrubbery, bushes.
Gestrüpp', n., bushes, thicket.
gesund', sound, healthy.
Gesund'heit, f., health.
getreu', true, faithful.
getrost', cheerfully, confidently.
gewah'ren, to see, perceive, be
aware.
gewäh'ren, to grant, yield.
Gewalt', f., force.

gewalt′fam, violently; with violence.

Gewäf′fer, *n.*, waters.

Gewehr′, *n.*, gun.

gewe′fen, (*p. p.*), been.

gewiß′, sure.

gewöh′nen, to accustom.

gewöhu′lich, usual, common.

Gewöl′be, *n.*, (arched) vault.

gewölbt′, (*p. p.*), arched, bent.

gewor′den, (*p. p.*), become.

gie′ßen (goß — gegoffen), to pour.

Gift, *n.*, poison.

Gip′fel, *m.*, top, peak.

Git′ter, *n.*, grate, rails.

Git′terfenfter, *n.*, lattice-window.

glän′zen, to shine, glitter.

gläu′zend, glittering, brilliant, glorious.

Glas′fchale, *f.*, glass-bowl.

glatt, smooth.

Glau′be(n), *m.*, belief, faith; superstition.

glau′ben, to believe, think.

gleich, like, resembling.

gleich′falls, likewise.

gleich′wohl, nevertheless.

glei′ten (glitt — geglitten), to glide.

Glet′fcher, *m.*, glacier.

Glied, *n.*, limb.

Glo′cke, *f.*, bell.

Glo′ckenblume, *f.*, bluebell, *bot.* Campanula.

Glo′rie, *f.*, glory.

Glück, *n.*, fortune, good luck, success.

glu′cken, to cluck.

Gluck′henne, *f.*, clucking hen.

glück′lich, fortunate, successful.

glü′hen, to glow.

Goe′the, Gœthe (poet).

Gold, *n.*, gold.

gol′den, of gold, golden.

Gold′fifchchen, *n.*, (little) gold-fish.

gold′lockig, with golden locks or curls.

Golf, *m.*, gulf, bay.

Gol′gatha, Golgotha.

Gon′del, *f.*, gondola.

Gott, *m.*, God. (*plu.*, die Götter, gods).

Got′tesacker, *m.*, cemetery.

Got′teshaus, *n.*, house of God, church, temple.

Gott′heit, *f.*, deity, idol.

Göt′tin, *f.*, goddess.

Grab, *n.*, grave.

Gra′ben, *m.*, ditch, moat.

Gra′bgewölbe, *n.*, vault, tomb.

Gra′feukrone, *f.*, earl's coronet.

Gras, *n.*, grass.

grau, gray.

grau′grün, grayish-green.

grei′fen (griff — gegriffen), to grasp; an die Thür greifen, to grasp the handle of the door.

grell, glaring, strong, loud.

Grie′che, *m.*, Greek.

Grie′chenknabe, *m.*, Greek boy.

grim′mig, grim, fierce.

Grön′land, Greenland.

Grön′länder, *m.*, Greenlander, Eskimo.

grön′läudifch, Greenlandish, of Greenland.

groß, great; large, huge; **etwas Großes,** something great.
Grö'ße, f., size; greatness.
Groß'mutter, f., grandmother.
grü'beln, to brood; **das Grübeln,** brooding.
grün, green.
Grund, m., ground; reason, cause; **vom Grunde auf,** up from the ground.
Grup'pe, f., group.
Gruß, m., greeting.
gu'cken, to look.
Guirlan'de, f., garland.
Gür'tel, m., belt.
gut, good; well.
Guts'besitzer, m., land-holder, proprietor of an estate.

H.

Haar, n., hair.
ha'ben (hatte — gehabt), to have.
halb, half.
halb'erwachsen, half-grown.
halb'geöffnet, half-opened.
Hal'le, f., hall.
hal'len, to sound, resound, echo.
Halt, m., stop; **halt machen,** to stop.
hal'ten (hielt — gehalten), to hold, take, keep; think, believe.
Ham'burg, Hamburg (city).
Hand, f., hand.
han'gen (hing — gehangen), (intrans.), to hang, be suspended, be perched.
hän'gen, (transit.), to suspend, place, put; often used for hangen.
Har'fe, f., harp.
Har'lekin, m., harlequin.
hart, hard, severe.
Ha'se, m., hare.
Ha'senpfote, f., hare's foot.
Häß'lichkeit, f., ugliness; **Schönheit und Häßlichkeit,** beauty and beast.
hau'chen, to breathe.
Hau'fen, m., heap, pile.
Haus, n., house; theatre.
Haus'gerät, n., household furniture.
Haus'klingel, f., door-bell.
häus'lich, domestic.
Haut, f., skin; a very thin skin stretched over the window-holes in the tents of the Greenlanders.
he'ben (hob — gehoben), to raise, lift up; **sich heben,** to rise, heave.
He'cke, f., hedge.
hef'ten, to fasten.
hef'tig, violent, fierce.
Hei'de, f., heath.
Hei'dekraut, n., heather.
Hei'delbeerkraut, n., bilberry-bush
hei'lig, holy, sacred.
Hei'mat, f., home.
hei'raten, to marry.
heiß, hot; ardent, passionate.
hei'ßen (hieß — geheißen), to be called, named; to mean; **das heißt,** that means, that is.
Hei'terkeit, f., cheerfulness.
Held, m., hero.

helʼfen (half — geholfen), to help, assist.

hell, clear, bright.

Hemd, *n*., shirt, chemise.

Henʼne, *f*., hen.

her, (*place:*) hither; (*time:*) ago.

herabʼ*blicken, to look down.

herabʼ*fliegen (flog — geflogen), to fly down, be thrown off.

herabʼ*hängen (hing — gehangen), to hang down.

herabʼ*sehen (sah — gesehen), to look down.

herabʼ*strecken, to stretch down.

herausʼ*führen, to set at liberty, release.

herausʼ*kriechen (kroch — gekrochen), to creep (crawl) from.

herausʼ*rufen (rief — gerufen), to call out.

herausʼ*stecken, to put out.

herausʼ*tragen (trug — getragen), to (take) carry out from.

herausʼ*treten (trat — getreten), to step forward.

herbeiʼ*rufen (rief — gerufen), to call to come near.

hereinʼ*schauen, to look (gaze) into.

hereinʼ*scheinen (schien — geschienen), to shine into.

herniederʼ*blicken, to look down.

heroʼisch, heroic; das Heroische, the heroic.

Herr, *m*., master, ruler; gentleman, Mr.

herrʼlich, masterly; magnificent.

Herrʼlichkeit, *f*., glory, majesty.

Herrʼschaft, *f*., (lord and lady), persons of rank; traveling party.

herrʼschen, to reign, rule, prevail, be.

herumʼ*flattern, to flutter around.

herumʼ*kriechen (kroch — gekrochen), to crawl around.

herumʼ*rühren, to stir about (up).

herumʼ*schwimmen (schwamm — geschwommen), to swim about.

herumʼ*springen (sprang — gesprungen), to (jump) spring about.

herumʼ*ziehen (zog — gezogen), to move about, wander.

herunʼter, down.

herunʼter*blicken, to look down.

herunʼter*brennen (brannte — gebrannt), to burn down.

herunʼterfallen (fiel — gefallen), to fall down, be cast down.

herunʼter*hängen (hing — gehangen), to hang down.

herunʼter*helfen (half — geholfen), to help down.

hervorʼ*blicken, to look (peep) from behind.

hervorʼ*blühen, to bloom forth.

hervorʼ*ragen, to project over, rise above.

hervorʼ*sehen (sah — gesehen), to look from behind.

hervorʼ*springen (sprang — gesprungen), to come forth, take rise.

Herz, *n*., heart; etwas über das Herz bringen, to bring one's self to do.

herz′lich, hearty, cordial.

heu′len, to howl, yell.

heu′te, to-day; heute Nacht, to-night.

Hia′tus, *m.*, hiatus.

hier, here.

hier′her, hither, here.

hilf′los, helpless, destitute.

Him′mel, *m.*, heaven.

himm′lisch, heavenly, celestial.

hinab′*senken, to send down.

hinauf′*klettern, to climb up.

hinauf′*kommen (kam — gekommen), to come up (stairs).

hinauf′*steigen (stieg — gestiegen), to ascend.

hinaus′*blicken, to look out.

hinaus′*rollen, to roll out of.

hinaus′*sehen (sah — gesehen), to look out.

(sich) hin′*biegen (bog — gebogen), to be bent toward.

Hin′du = Mädchen, *n.*, Hindoo-girl.

hindurch′*blicken, to look through.

hinein′*blicken, to look, (gaze) into.

hinein′*schlüpfen, to slip into.

hin′*fahren (fuhr — gefahren), to ride (drive) along.

hin′*gehen (ging — gegangen), to go along.

hin′ken, to limp.

hin′*laufen (lief — gelaufen), to run along, stretch along.

hin′*schleichen (schlich — geschlichen), to steal up to.

hin′*schreiben (schrieb — geschrieben), to write down.

hin′*setzen, to put down; sich hinsetzen, to seat one's self.

hin′*sterben (starb — gestorben), to die away.

hin′ten, back.

hin′ter, behind, back.

Hin′terfuß, *m.*, hind-foot.

Hin′tergrund, *m.*, background.

hinterher′*laufen (lief — gelaufen), to run after (behind them).

hin und her, hither and thither.

hin und wieder, here and there; now and then.

hinun′ter*blicken, to look down.

hinun′ter*fliegen (flog — geflogen), to be cast down, fly from.

hinun′ter*schauen, to gaze down.

(sich) hinun′ter*schleichen (schlich — geschlichen), to steal down (stairs).

hinweg′*blicken, to look over.

hinweg′*fliegen (flog — geflogen), to fly along over.

hinweg′*jagen, to chase away, hurry away.

hinweg′*schwimmen (schwamm — geschwommen), to swim along over.

hinweg′*ziehen (zog — gezogen), to pass over.

hin′*ziehen (zog — gezogen), to pass along.

hinzu′*fügen, to add.

hinzu′*setzen, to add.

Histo′rie, *f.*, story.

hoch, high.

Hoch, *n.*, cheer; hurrah!

Hoch'altar, *m.*, high-altar.

Hoch'zeit, *f.*, wedding.

Hoch'zeitstag, *m.*, day of wedding.

Hö'cker, *m.*, hump.

Hof, *m.*, court, yard.

Hohe, *n.*, the high; what is high.

Höhe, *f.*, height. in die Höhe, up.

höher, higher.

höh'nisch, scornful.

hold, charming, sweet.

Holz, *n.*, wood.

hölzern, of wood, wooden.

Holz'stift, *m.*, wooden peg (pin).

Holz'stoß, *m.*, pile of wood.

Holzwerk, *n.*, wood-work.

hor'chen, to listen.

hö'ren, to hear.

Horizont', *m.*, horizon.

Horn, *n.*, horn, bugle; cusp of the crescent moon.

hübsch, pretty, nice; a great deal.

Huf'schlag, *m.*, hoof-stroke.

Hü'gel, *m.*, hill.

Hüh'nerhaus, *n.*, hen-coop.

hul'digen, to pay homage.

Hul'digung, *f.*, homage.

hül'len, to wrap up; sich hüllen, to cover one's self.

Hund, *m.*, dog.

Hünd'chen, *n.*, little dog.

hun'dert, hundred; Hunderte, hundreds.

Hü'nengrab, *n.*, giant's grave.

hüp'fen, to hop, leap.

Hut, *m.*, hat.

Hut'filz, *m.*, hatters' felt.

Hüt'te, *f.*, hut.

Hym'ne, *f.*, hymn, song.

J.

ich, I.

Ideal', *n.*, ideal.

Idee', *f.*, idea.

ihm, (*dat.*), him, (to, for, with) him.

ihn, (*accus.*), him.

ih'nen, them; to, for them.

Ih'nen, (*dat.*), you, (to, for, with) you.

ihr, (*dat.*), her (to, for, with) her; *possess. pron.*, her, hers.

ih'ren, (*accus.*), her.

Ih'rige, (*nom. and accus.*), yours.

im = in dem, in the.

im'mer, always.

im'merhin, after all.

Immortel'lenkranz, *m.*, wreath of immortelles.

improvisie'ren, to improvise, extemporize.

in, in; into.

indem', while.

In'dien, India.

in'digofarben, Indigo-blue.

In'halt, *m.*, contents.

In'nere, *n.*, interior; mind, intellect.

in'nerhalb, inside (of), within.

in'nig, warm; deep.

In'sel, *f.*, island.

Interpunktion', *f.*, punctuation.

ir'ben, earthen.

ir'bifdy, earthly.

ir'genb, ever, soever, any; irgenb einer, anyone.

ir'genbwo, somewhere; anywhere.

Is'rael, Israel; das Volk Israel, children of Israel.

J.

ja, yes; you know; why; even.

Jagb, f., chase.

ja'gen, to chase.

Jahr, n., year; Jahr aus, Jahr ein, year by year.

Jahrhun'bert, n., a hundred years, century.

Jahrtau'fenb, n., a thousand years.

Jaloufie', f., Venetian blind.

Jam'mer, m., grief, wailing.

jäm'merlidy, pitiable, miserable.

jaudy'zen, to shout for joy, exult.

je'ber, jebe, jebes, each, every.

je'besmal, each time.

je'manb, some one.

je'ner, jene, jenes, that.

jen'feits, on the other side.

Je'fustinb, n., child Jesus.

jetzt, now.

Jod, n., yoke.

Ju'bel, m., shout of joy, loud rejoicing.

ju'beln, to rejoice loudly.

Ju'belton, m., expression of joy.

Ju'be, m., Jew.

Ju'bengaffe, f., Jews' Quarters; "Ghetto".

Ju'genb, f., youth; vigor of youth.

ju'genblidy, youthful.

Ju'lirevolution, f., July revolution.

jung, young.

Jun'ge, m., boy, lad.

Jung'fer, f., maiden.

Jüng'ling, m., youth, young man.

K.

Kabett', m., cadet.

Kahn, m., canoe, boat.

Kai'ferburg, f., palace of the Caesars.

Kai'fertrönuug, f., coronation of an emperor.

Ka'jat, m., Kajak (Kayak).

talt, cold.

Käl'te, f., cold.

Kamel', n., camel.

Kamerab', m., comrade; play fellow.

Kamin', m., chimney.

Kam'mer, f., (small) room.

Käm'merchen, n., (small) room.

Kampf, m., fight.

täm'pfen, to fight.

Käm'pfenbe, m., combatant.

Ka'naan, Canaan.

Kapel'le, f., chapel.

Kapitäl', n., capital.

Karawa'ne, f., caravan.

Kar'ren, m., cart.

Kar'te, f., card.

Käft'chen, n., little chest.

Kattun', m., cotton (cloth), calico

tau'ern, to couch.

kaufen, to buy.

Kaufmann, m., merchant.

kaum, hardly, scarcely.

keck, pert, bold, fearless.

kehren, to turn.

kein, no.

keinesfalls, by no means.

kennen (kannte — gekannt), to know.

Kerze, f., taper, wax-light.

Kind, n., child.

Kinn, n., chin.

Kirche, f., church.

Kirchengemälde, n., church-painting.

Kirchhof, m., church-yard.

Kirchhofsmauer, f., wall of the church-yard.

Klafter, f., cord, fathom.

klafterlang, a fathom (= 6 feet) long.

klar, clear, bright.

Klasse, f., class.

klatsch! whick-whack!

Kleid, n., dress.

kleiden, to dress.

Kleidung, f., clothes.

klein, little, small; der, (die, das) Kleine, little one.

klettern, to climb.

Klingel, f., bell.

Klingelzug, m., bell-string.

klingen (klang — geklungen), to sound.

klingling! ding ting!

klirrend, jingling, crashing.

klopfen, to club, knock.

Kloster, n., cloister, convent.

Klosterkirche, f., conventual church.

Knabe, m., boy.

knallen, to crack.

Knecht, m., male-servant.

Knie, n., knee.

knien, to kneel.

Knopf, m., button.

knüpfen, to entwine.

Kobold, m., goblin, gnome.

kolossal', colossal.

komisch, comic, funny; wird komisch, is funny.

kommen (kam — gekommen), to come.

Komödie, f., comedy, play.

König, m., king.

Königin, f., queen.

königlich, royal.

Königreich, n., kingdom.

Königskrone, f., royal crown.

können (pres., kann, impf. konnte, pp. gekonnt), to be able.

Kopenhagen, Copenhagen.

Kopf, m., head.

Köpfchen, n., little head.

Kopfputz, m., head-dress.

Koran', m., Koran; Al-Koran.

Körper, m., body.

kostbar, precious, costly.

kosten, to cost.

krachen, to crack.

kräftig, strong, robust.

Kranich, m., crane.

krank, sick; der Kranke, sick man

Kranz, m., wreath, crown.

Krater, m., crater; vacant space

(ſich) **krän′ſeln,** to curl, ripple.
krei′beweiß, white as chalk; quite
  pale.
Kreis, *m.,* circle.
Kreis′gang, *m.,* circular motion;
  customary motion; orbit.
Kreſ′ſe, *f.,* cress, cresses.
Kreuz, *n.,* cross.
kreu′zen, to cross.
krie′chen (kroch — gekrochen), to
  creep, crawl.
Krie′ger, *m.,* warrior.
Krip′pe, *f.,* crib.
Krokodil′, *n.*. crocodile.
Kro′ne, *f.,* crown, top.
Kron′leuchter, *m.,* chandelier.
Krug, *m.,* pitcher, jug.
Küch′lein, *n.,* little chicken.
Kuck′uck, *m.,* cuckoo.
Ku′gel, *f.,* ball, globe, sphere.
küh′len, to cool.
kühn, bold, reckless.
Kum′mer, *m.,* grief, sorrow.
küm′mern, to care.
Kun′de, *f.,* news.
Kunſt, *f.,* art.
kup′fern, of copper.
Kup′pel, *f.,* cupola, dome.
kurz, short.
Kuß, *m.,* kiss.
küſ′ſen, to kiss.
Kuß′hand, *f.,* kiss; jemandem Kuß-
  hände zuwerfen, to kiss one's
  hand to one.
Kü′ſte, f., coast.
Kut′ſcher, m., coachman, driver.

L.

la′chen, to laugh; das Lachen, laugh
  ing, laughter.
lä′cheln, to smile; das Lächeln, smile.
lä′cherlich, ridiculous.
lackie′ren, to lacker, varnish.
La′is, Lais.
Land, *n.,* land, country.
Lam′pe, *f.,* lamp.
Land′leute, *plu.,* country-people,
  peasants.
Land′ſee, *m.,* lake.
Land′ſtraße, *f.,* highway.
lang, long.
lan′ge, (*adv.*) for a long time.
Langewei′le, *f.,* weariness, ennui.
längs, alongside of, along.
lang′ſam, slow.
(am) **läng′ſten,** the longest.
Lao′koon, Laocöon.
Läpp′chen, *n.,* (little) rag.
Lap′pen, *m.,* rag.
laſ′ſen (ließ — gelaſſen), to let,
  cause; = zulaſſen, zugeben, to admit, concede.
Laſt, *f.,* burden.
lau′ern, to lie in wait, lurk.
lau′fen (lief — gelaufen), to run.
Lau′ge, *f.,* (lye); bitter censure, criticism.
Lau′ne, *f.,* freak, whim, caprice.
lau′ſchen, to listen.
laut, loud, aloud.
läu′ten, (*trans.*), to ring the bell;
  (*intrans.*), to ring, sound (of
  bells).

laut′los, silent.

La′va, *f.*, lava.

La′vastein, *m.*, lava-rock.

Lazzaro′ne, *m.*, lazzarone; tramp.

le′ben, to live, be alive. lebend, living, alive; lebende Bilder, "tableaux vivants", = living pictures, representation of some scene by groups of persons.

Le′ben, *n.*, life.

leben′dig, living.

Lebewohl′, *n.*, farewell.

leer, empty.

lee′ren, to empty, drain.

le′gen, to lay, put, place.

Lehm, *m.*, clay.

(sich) leh′nen, to lean, recline.

Lehn′sessel, *m.*, arm-chair.

Lei′che, *f.*, corpse.

Lei′chenwagen, *m.*, hearse.

leicht, light, merry, nimble.

Leich′tigkeit, *f.*, ease.

Leib, *n.*, harm; zu leibe thuen, to harm, hurt.

lei′den (litt — gelitten), to suffer.

Lei′den, *n.*, suffering.

Lei′ne, *f.*, cord, rope.

leis, soft, feeble.

lei′se, (*adv.*), gently, quietly.

Ler′che, *f.*, lark.

ler′nen, to learn, study

le′sen, (las — gelesen), to read.

letzt, last.

letzt′vergangen, (very) last, just passed.

leuch′ten, *to* shine, beam.

Leuch′ter, *m.*, candlestick.

Leu′te, (*plu.*), people.

Lia′ne, *f.*, liana.

licht, bright, clear.

Licht, *n.*, light.

lieb, dear, beloved.

Lie′be, *f.*, love.

lie′ben, to love.

lie′ber, rather, better; lieber sein, to like better, prefer.

Lie′besgott, *m.*, god of love, Cupid.

lieb′lich, charming, sweet.

Lieb′ling, *m.*, favorite, pet.

liebst, best, kindest.

(am) lieb′sten, best; wollte am lieb-sten, liked best.

Lied, *n.*, song.

lie′fern, to furnish, give.

lie′gen (lag — gelegen), to lie, be placed.

li′la, lilac.

Li′lie, *f.*, lily.

Lip′pe, *f.*, lip.

lis′peln, to whisper.

Lob, *n.*, praise.

lo′ben, to praise.

Loch, *n.*, hole.

lo′ckig, curly.

Lo′ge, (French!) *f.*, box (in the theatre.)

Lor′beer, *m.*, laurel.

Lor′beerstrauch, *m.*, laurel-tree.

los′*reißen (riß — gerissen), to tear from.

Lo′tosblume, *f.*, water-lily.

Lou′vre, *m.*, Louvre.

Lö′we, *m.*, lion.

Luft, *f.*, air, atmosphere.

Lüft'chen, *n.*, breeze, zephyr.
luf'tig, airy.
Luft'raum, *m.*, atmosphere.
Luft'zug, *m.*, draught of air, current of air.
lu'gen, to look, peep.
Lu'te, *f.*, window-hole, (in a stable), shutter.
Lum'pen, *m.*, rag.
Lü'neburg, Lüneburg (town).
Luft, *f.*, desire.
Luft'barkeit, *f.*, sport, merriment.
lu'ftig, merry, funny.
Lych'nis, *f.*, Lychnis (plant).

M.

Mäcen', *m.*, Maecenas; protector, patron.
ma'chen, to make.
Macht, *f.*, might, splendor.
mäch'tig, mighty, powerful, strong.
Mäd'chen, *n.*, girl
Magd, *f.*, servant girl.
ma'ger, meager lean, thin.
Mäh'ne, *f.*, mane.
mä'teln, to find fault.
Mal (mal), *n.*, time.
ma'len, to paint, sketch.
Ma'ler, *m.*, painter.
Ma'ma, *f.*, mamma.
man, one, we, they people.
manch, many a.
manch'mal, sometimes.
Mann, *m.*, man.
Man'tel, *m.*, mantel, cloak.
Mär'chen, *n.*, story, fairy-tale, legend.

Markt, *m.*, market, fair.
Mar'mor, *m.*, marble.
Mar'morbecken, *n.*, marble-basin.
Mar'morbild, *n.*, marble-picture.
Marmorflie'se, *f.*, marble-flag-stone.
Mar'morgott, *m.*, marble-statue of a god.
mar'morn, of marble.
Mar'morsäule, *f.*, marble-column, pillar.
Marsch, *m.*, march.
marschie'ren, to march.
Maschinist', *m.*, scene-shifter.
Mas'se, *f.*, mass.
Mast, *m.*, mast.
matt, dim, faint.
Mau'er, *f.*, wall.
Maul, *n.*, mouth; tongue.
Maul'trommel, *f.*, Jew's harp.
Mausole'um, *n.*, mausoleum.
Meer *n.*, ocean, sea.
Meer'busen, *m.*, gulf, bay.
Mee'resfläche, *f.*, surface of the sea.
Mee'resspiegel, *m.*, surface of the sea.
mehr, more.
meh'rere, several.
Mei'le, *f.*, mile.
mein, my.
mei'nen, to mean, think, remark.
Mei'nung, *f.*, opinion.
meist, most.
Melancholie', *f.*, meloncholy, sadness.
melancho'lisch, melancholy, sad.
Melodie', *f.*, melody.

Menſch, *m.*, man.

Men'ſchenſeele, *f.*, human soul.

mer'fen, to notice.

merf'würdig, remarkable.

Meſ'ſer, *n.*, knife.

Meſ'ſingſcheibe, *f.*, brass-plate, brass-disk.

Met'horn, *n.*, mead-horn.

mich, (*accus.*), me.

Mimo'ſe, *f.*, mimosa.

Minn'te, *f.*, minute.

mir, (*dat.*), me, (to, for, by) me.

(ſich) mi'ſchen, to be mingled.

mit, with, together with.

Mit'telmäßigfeit, *f.*, mediocrity.

mit'ten, in the midst of.

Mit'ternacht, *f.*, midnight.

mitun'ter, occasionally, now and then.

mit'*weinen, to cry together with (one).

Mö'bel, *plu.*, furniture.

Mo'be, *f.*, fashion.

mö'gen (*pres.*, mag; *impf.*, mochte; *p. p.*, gemocht), may.

Moment', *m.*, moment, minute.

Mo'nat, *m.*, month.

Mond, *m.*, moon.

Monument', *n.*, monument.

Moor, *n.*, moor, swamp.

Moos, *n.*, moss.

moos'bewachſen, moss-covered.

Moral', *f.*, moral, lesson.

mor'gen, to-morrow.

Mor'gen, *m.*, morning.

Mor'gendämmerung, *f.*, dawn, morning-twilight.

Mor'gengeſang, *m.*, morning-song.

Mor'genrot, *n.*, morning-red, dawn, aurora.

Mor'genröte, *f.*, dawn, rosy morn.

Mor'genwolfe, *f.*, morning-cloud.

Mül'ler, *m.*, miller; des Müller's Chriſtine, Christina, the miller's daughter.

Mund, *m.*, mouth.

Mu'ſchel, *f.*, shell.

Mu'ſe, *f.*, Muse.

Muſif', *f.*, music.

Muſifau'tenfamilie, *f.*, a musician's family.

müſ'ſen (*pres.*, muß; *impf.*, mußte; *p. p.*, gemußt), to must, have to, be compelled.

Mut, *m.*, courage; es iſt mir zu Mute, I feel.

mu'tig, courageous, spirited, mettle-some.

Mut'ter, *f.*, mother.

Mut'terherz, *n.*, mother's heart.

Müt'ze, *f.*, cap.

N.

nach, (*prepos.*), after, at, toward, for.

Nach'bar, *m.*, neighbor.

nachdem' (*conj.*), after.

nach'*denfen (dachte — gedacht), to think over, reflect.

nach'*geben (gab — gegeben), to yield.

nach'her, afterwards.

Nach'läſſigfeit, *f.*, blunder.

nach'ſichtig, indulgent, lenient.

Nacht, f., night.

Nacht'hembchen, n., little night-shirt.

Nach'tigall, f., nightingale.

nackt, bare, naked.

Nackt'heit, f., bareness, nakedness.

na'h(e), near; nahe bei, near by.

Nä'he, f., neighborhood.

nahen, to approach, come near.

nähen, to sew.

(sich) nä'hern, to come near, approach.

Nah'rung, f., food, nourishment.

Na'me(n), m., name.

na'mentlich, especially.

Napo'leon, Napoléon Bonaparte.

Naß, n., fluid, liquor.

Natur', f., nature.

Nea'pel, Naples (town).

neapolita'nisch, Neapolitan.

Ne'bel, m., fog, mist.

ne'ben, beside.

nebenher', along with, by the side of.

Ne'ger, m., negro.

Ne'gerschar, f., troop, crowd of negroes.

neh'men (nahm — genommen), to take, seize.

(sich) nei'gen, to bow, bend.

nein, no.

nen'nen (nannte — genannt), to name, call.

Nest, n., nest.

Netz, n., net, net-work.

neu, new, other; aufs neue, anew.

'eunt, ninth.

neun'zehnt, nineteenth.

nicht, not.

(mit) nich'ten, by no means.

nichts, nothing.

ni'cken, to nod.

nie, never.

nie'der, down.

nie'der*blicken, to look down.

nie'der*lächeln, to smile down.

(sich) nie'der*setzen, to seat one's self.

nie'der*treten (trat — getreten), to tread (stamp) down.

nied'lich, pretty.

nied'rig, low.

nie'mand, no one, nobody.

Nil, m., Nile.

Nil'gruppe, f., Nile group.

Ni'sche, f., niche.

Ni'zenblume, f., water-lily.

No'ah, Noah.

noch, still, yet; noch ein, still another.

noch'mals, once more.

Non'ne, f., nun.

Non'nenkloster, n., nunnery.

Nord'licht, n., Northern lights.

Nord'lichtkrone, f., "Aurora borealis."

Not, f., distress, need.

No'te, f., musical note.

notie'ren, to note, take down.

nö'tig, needy, necessary; nötig haben, to need.

nun, now, just, well.

nur, only.

O.

ob, if, whether.
o'ben, up, above, on the top, up stairs.
obgleich', although.
Obſt'garten, *m.*, orchard.
obwohl', although.
Och'ſe, *m.*, ox.
o'der, or.
O'din, Odin (Northern deity).
of'fen, open, public.
Offizier', *m.*, officer (of the army).
öff'nen, to open.
oft, often.
oh! o!
oh'ne, without.
Op'fer, *n.*, bribe, fee.
Orche'ſter, *n.*, orchestra.
or'dentlich, proper, regular.
Orientaliſt', *m.*, orientalist.
Ort, *m.*, place, spot.
öſt'lich, Eastern.

P.

Paar, *n.*, pair, couple.
Pagi'na, *f.*, page.
Pal'me, *f.*, palm-tree.
Papier' *n.*, paper.
Paris' Paris (city).
Paſſagier' (French!) *m.*, passenger.
Pa'thos, *n.*, pathos.
Pe, Pe (girls' name).
Peit'ſche, *f.*, whip.
peit'ſchen, to whip.
Pe'likan, *m.*, pelican.
Pelz, *m.*, fur-coat.

Perpendi'kel, *m.*, pendulum; perpendicle.
Perſon', *f.*, person.
Pe'terskirche, *f.*, St. Peter's Church.
Petz, *m.*, "Sir Bruin."
Pfei'fe, *f.*, pipe; whistle.
pfei'fen, to whistle.
Pfeil, *m.*, arrow fish-spear.
Pferd, *n.*, horse; zu Pferd, on horseback.
pfif'fig, clever.
Pflan'ze, *f.*, plant.
pfla'ſtern, to pave.
pfle'gen, to be accustomed, use to.
Phantaſie', *f.*, fantasy, fancy.
phanta'ſtiſch, fantastic.
pi'cken, to pick.
Pi'nie, *f.*, stone-pine.
Plata'ne, *f.* plane-tree.
plät'ſchern, to splash.
Platz, *m.*, place, seat; Platz nehmen, to seat one's self.
plump, heavy, clumsy.
Pö'bel, *m.*, populace, mob.
Poeſie', *f.*, poesy poetry.
Polar'vogel, *m.*, polar-bird, fulmar.
Polichinell' *m* Punch, clown.
Polizei' *f.*, police.
Pompe'ji, Pompeii.
Porzellan', *n.*, porcelain.
poſſier'lich, comic, droll.
Poſt'horn, *n.*, postillion's bugle.
Po'ſtillion, *m.*, postillion.
Pracht, *f.*, splendor, magnificence.
Pracht'anzug, *m.*, rich dress, state-dress.
präch'tig, splendid, magnificent.

pran'gen, to shine, display splendor.
preis'*geben (gab — gegeben), to sacrifice to, give up.
Prophet', *m.,* prophet.
prophezei'en, to foretell, prophesy.
Provinzial'städtchen, *n.,* provincial town.
Pub'likum, *n.,* public, audience.
Pult, *n.,* desk.
Punkt, *m.,* point, spot.
Pup'pe, *f.,* doll.
Pur'pur, *m.,* purple.
pur'purn, purple.
Pur'purteppich, *m.,* purple-carpet, purple-tapestry.
pu'tzen, to adorn.

Q.

quer, across.

R.

Rad, *n.,* wheel.
ra'gen, to project, tower up.
Rand, *m.,* edge.
Ra'sen, *m.,* turf.
Rat'haus, *n.,* city-hall.
Rauch, *m.,* smoke.
rau'chen, to smoke.
Rauch'wolke, *f.,* cloud of smoke.
Raum, *m.,* space.
rau'schen, to rustle.
Recension', *f.,* review, criticism.
recht, right, very, quiet, exactly; recht viel, a good deal).
Redacteur', *m.,* editor (of a news-paper).

Re'de, *f.,* talk; es kann keine Rede davon sein, it is out of question.
red'lich, honest.
Regisseur' (French!), *m.,* (theatrical) manager.
rei'ben (rieb — gerieben), to rub.
reich, rich, luxuriant.
Reich, *n.,* empire, realm.
rei'chen, to offer, reach.
reich'gemalt, richly painted.
reich'lich, plenty, sufficient.
Rei'he, *f.,* line, order; außer der Reihe, at random.
rein, pure, clean.
Rei'se, *f.,* travel, trip, journey.
rei'sen, to travel.
Rei'sende, *m. and f.,* traveler.
Rei'sewagen, *m.,* traveling coach.
rei'ßen (riß — gerissen), to tear.
rei'ten (ritt — geritten), to ride on horseback.
rei'zend, sweet, charming.
(sich) rich'ten, to direct one's way.
Rie'gel, *m.,* bolt.
rie'senhaft, gigantic.
Ring, *m.,* ring.
rings, around.
rings'um, round about.
Rit'ter, *m.,* knight; hero.
rit'terlich, knightly, heroic.
Rit'tersitz, *m.,* nobleman's castle.
ri'tzen, to scratch.
Rock, *m.,* coat, petticoat.
roh, rude.
Rol'le, *f.,* part, character.
rol'len, to roll.
Rom (Ro'ma), Rome (Roma).

Ro′meo, Romeo.

ro′fa, rose-colored.

Ro′fa-Hut, *m.,* pink-trimmed hat.

Ro′fe, *f.,* rose.

Roß, *n.,* horse, steed.

Roffi′ni, Rossini.

rö′ften, to roast.

rot, red.

Roth′fchild, Rothschild (family-name).

Ro′xen, *m.,* Lake Roxen (Sweden).

Rü′cken, *m.,* back.

ru′fen (rief — gerufen), to call out, exclaim.

Ru′he, *f.,* rest, repose, quiet; zur Ruhe bringen, to lay (put) down.

ru′hen, to rest, repose.

ru′hig, quiet, calm.

rüh′ren, to stir.

Rui′ne, *f.,* ruins.

rund, round.

Ruß, *m.,* soot.

S.

Saal, *m.* (*plu.,* Säle), hall.

Sa′che, *f.,* matter, thing, affair.

Säck′chen, *n.,* little bag.

fä′en, to sow.

fa′gen, to say.

Salz, *n.,* salt.

Salz′ebene, *f.,* salt-plain.

fam′meln, to gather, collect.

Samt, *m.,* velvet.

Sand, *m.,* sand.

Sanda′le, *f.,* sandal.

Sand′hügel, *m.,* sand-hill.

Sand′meer, *n.,* sandy waste.

Sandfäule, *f.,* sand-spout.

Sand′wüfte, *f.,* sandy desert.

fanft, soft, mild, gentle.

Sän′ger, *m.,* singer, poet.

Sän′gerin, *f.,* female singer, songstress.

Sarg, *m.,* coffin.

Sat′tel, *m.,* saddle.

Satz, *m.,* leap.

Säu′le, *f.,* pillar, column.

fan′fen, to roar.

fcha′de! pity!

Schä′del, *m.,* skull.

fchaf′fen (fchuf — gefchaffen), to shape, create.

Schalmei′, *f.,* shawn, reedpipe.

Schan′ze, *f.,* bulwark.

Schar, *f.,* troop.

fcharf, sharp, clear.

fcharf′gezeichnet, sharply cut.

Schat′ten, *m.,* shadow, shade.

Schatz, *m.,* treasure.

fchau′en, to look, gaze.

fchän′men, to foam, froth.

Schau′fpieler, *m.,* actor.

Schei′be, *f.,* disk; window-pane.

fchei′nen (fchien — gefchienen), to shine, seem, appear.

fchel′mifch, roguish.

fchel′ten (fchalt — gefcholten), to scold, censure.

Sche′mel, *m.,* foot-stool.

Schen′ke, *f.,* inn, tavern.

fchen′ken, to give, present.

fcher′zen, to joke, jest; im Scherz, jokingly, for fun.

fcheu, shy, timid.

schief, inclined, sloping, slanting.

schie'ßen (schoß — geschossen), to shoot.

Schiff, n., ship, boat.

Schild, n., sign-board.

Schildkrötenschale, f., tortoise-shell.

Schilf, n., reeds, rushes.

schim'mern, to glisten, glimmer

Schirm, m., screen, protection; zu einem Schirm, like a screen.

Schlä'fe, f., temple (of the head).

schla'fen (schlief — geschlafen), to sleep.

Schlag, m. (= Wagenschlag), carriage-door.

schla'gen (schlug — geschlagen), to strike; to sing, warble.

Schlagschatten, m., dark shade.

Schlan'ge, f., serpent, snake.

schlank, slender, straight.

Schlehdorn, m., black-thorn.

(sich) schlei'chen (schlich — geschli= chen) to steal, sneak.

schlie'ßen (schloß geschlossen), to shut, close, lock.

Schloß, n., lock.

schlum'mern, to slumber, sleep.

Schlüs'selloch, n., key-hole.

Schluß, m., close, end, conclusion.

schmal, narrow.

Schmerz, m., pain, grief.

schmerz'erfüllt, painful, agonized.

(sich) schmie'gen, to cling, nestle.

schmin'ken, to paint, powder (the face).

schmü'cken, to adorn.

Schna'bel, m., bill, beak.

schnau'ben, to snort.

Schnee, m., snow.

schnee'weiß, snow-white.

schnell, swift, fast, quick.

Schnur, f., cord, belt.

schnur'ren, to hum.

schon, already.

schön, beautiful, fair.

Schön'heit, f., beauty.

Schorn'stein, m., chimney.

Schorn'steinfegerjunge, m., chimney-sweeper's apprentice.

Schoß, m., lap, knees.

Schreck, m., fright, terror

schre'cklich, terrible, frightful.

schreib'en (schrieb — geschrieben), to write.

schrei'en (schrie — geschrieen), to cry out; scream.

schrei'ten (schritt — geschritten), to step.

Schrift'steller, m., author.

Schritt, m., step.

Schuh, m., shoe.

Schuld, f., guilt; daran sind schuld, for that are to be blamed.

Schul'ter, f., shoulder.

Schup'pen, m., shed, repository.

Schutt, m., rubbish.

Schutt'haufen, m., heap of rubbish.

schüt'teln, to shake.

Schutz, m., protection.

schwach, weak, feeble, faint.

Schwal'bennest, n., swallow's nest.

Schwan, m., swan.

Schwarm, m flock.

schwarz, black; der Schwarze, negro.

schwär′zen, to blacken.
schwarz′gekleidet, dressed in black.
schwe′ben, to hover, soar.
Schwe′den, Sweden.
schwei′gen (schwieg — geschwiegen), to be silent.
schwel′len (schwoll — geschwollen), to swell.
schwer, heavy, difficult.
schwer′beladen, heavily-laden.
Schwert, n., sword.
Schwe′ster, f., sister.
schwim′men (schwamm — geschwommen), to swim, drift.
schwin′gen (schwang — geschwungen), to swing, wheel around.
sechs, six.
sechst, sixth.
sech′zehn, sixteen.
sech′zehnt, sixteenth.
See, f., sea, ocean.
See′hund, m., sea-dog; seal.
See′hundsfang, m., seal-fishing, hunting seals.
See′land, Zealand (island).
See′le, f., soul.
see′lenvergnügt, satisfied to one's heart's content.
see′lenvoll, soulful, feeling, wistful.
See′seite, f., sea-side; from the sea.
se′hen (sah — gesehen), to see, perceive.
Sehn′sucht, f., longing.
sehr, very, extremely.
sei, be! he may be.
Sei′de, f., silk.
Sei′denfranse, f., silken fringe.

Sei′fenblase, f., soap-bubble.
sein (pres., ich bin; impf., war; p.p., gewesen), to be.
sein, seine, sein (pron.), his.
sei′nige, his (own).
seit, since.
Sei′te, f., side; page.
selbst (him-, her-, it-, etc.), self.
Selbst′mord, m., suicide.
Selbst′mörder, m, suicide.
se′lig, happy, blissful.
Se′ligkeit, f., happiness, bliss.
selt′sam, strange, peculiar.
sen′den (sandte — gesandt), to send.
sen′ken, to sink, let down, lower.
se′tzen, to put, place; sich setzen, to seat one's self.
seuf′zen, to sigh.
Seuf′zerbrücke, f., "Bridge-of-Sighs."
Shawl, m., shawl.
sich (him-, her-, it-) self; (your-, them-) selves.
si′cher, sure, safe, true.
Si′cherheit, f., confidence.
sicht′bar, visible.
sie, she (her); they (them).
Sie, you.
sie′ben, seven.
sie′bent, seventh.
sieb′zehnt, seventeenth.
Sieg, m., victory.
Sie′gesmast, m., column of victory.
Sie′gestag, m., day of victory.
Sil′ber, n., silver.
sil′bern, silver, of silver.
Sil′berpapier, n., silver-paper.

fin'gen (fang — gefungen), to sing, warble.

fin'fen (fanf — gefunfen), to sink, fall.

Sinn, *m.*, mind, interest, sense.

fi'ßen (faß — gefeffen), to be seated, sit down.

Skiz'ze, *f.*, sketch.

fo, so, thus.

fobald', as soon.

fogar', even.

fogenannt', so-called.

Sohn, *m.*, son.

Soldat', *m.*, soldier.

Söld'ling, *m.*, mercenary soldier.

fol'len, to have to, must, ought.

Som'mer, *m.*, summer.

Som'mernacht, *f.*, summer-night.

Som'merrock, *m.*, summer-coat.

Som'merzelt, *n.*, summer-camp.

fon'derbar, strange, peculiar.

fon'dern, but.

Son'ne, *f.*, sun.

fonft, usually, formerly; else, otherwise.

Sorren'to, Sorrento (town).

Souffleur', (French!) *m.*, prompter.

Spal'te, *f.*, split, crack, crevice.

fpan'nen, to stretch.

Spar'ren, *m.*, rafter.

fpät, late; fpäter, later.

fpazie'ren gehen (ging — gegangen), to take a walk.

Spazier'fahrt, *f.*, pleasure-ride, pleasure-drive.

fpen'den, to give, bestow.

Sphinx, *f.*, Sphinx.

Spie'gel, *m.*, mirror, surface.

(fich) fpie'geln, to be reflected.

Spiel, *n.*, play, game; Spiel treiben, to play.

fpie'len, to play.

Spin'ne, *f.*, spider.

fpin'nen (fpann — gefponnen), to spin.

Spinn'rad, *n.*, spinning-wheel.

fpiß, pointed.

fpot'ten, to mock.

Spra'che, *f.*, language.

fpre'chen (fprach — gefprochen), to speak.

fprei'zen, to spread.

Spring'brunnen, *m.*, fountain.

fprin'gen (fprang — gefprungen), to spring, leap.

fpri'ßen, to spurt.

Spu'le, *f.*, spool.

Spur, *f.*, track.

Staat, *m.*, dress; finery.

Stab, *m.*, staff.

Stadt, *f.*, city, town.

Städt'chen, *n.*, little town.

Stall, *m.*, stable.

Stamm, *m.*, trunk; tribe.

Stand, *m.*, stall.

ftarf, strong.

ftär'fen, to strengthen.

ftatt, instead of.

Staub, *m.*, dust; spray.

fte'chen (ftach — geftochen), to thrust.

fte'cken, to stick.

fte'hen (ftand — geftanden), to stand; be; be written; fit; be becoming.

steif, stiff.

steigen (stieg — gestiegen), to ascend.

steil, steep.

Stein, *m.*, stone.

steinern, (of) stone.

Steinhaufen, *m.*, pile of stones.

Steinsarg, *m.*, (stone-coffin), sarcophagus.

Stelle, *f.*, place, spot.

stellen, to place, put.

stellenweise, here and there, in some places.

Stengel, *m.*, stalk.

sterben (starb — gestorben), to die.

sterblich, mortal; der Sterbliche, the mortal; man.

stets, always.

St. (= Sankt) Helena, St. Helena (island).

sticken, to embroider.

stier, staring.

Stift, *m.*, peg.

still, quiet, still; im stillen, quietly, secretly.

Stille, *f.*, stillness.

stillen, to quench.

Stirn, *f.*, forehead.

Stock, *m.*, stick.

Stöckchen, *n.*, little stick.

stoßen (stieß — gestoßen), to push, thrust.

straff, tight; straff angezogen, tightened, straightened.

Strahl, *m.*, beam, ray.

strahlen, to beam.

Strand, *m.*, strand, shore, beach.

Straße, *f.*, street.

sträuben, to erect (in bristles), bristle up.

straucheln, to stumble.

strecken, to stretch.

streichen (strich — gestrichen), to blow, sweep.

streicheln, to caress.

Stroh, *n.*, straw.

Strohdach, *n.*, thatched roof.

Strohdecke, *f.*, straw-mat.

Strohhut, *m.*, straw-hat.

Strom, *m.*, river.

strömen, to stream, flow.

Strumpf, *m.*, stocking.

Stube, *f.*, room.

Stück, *n.*, piece; drama, play.

Studium, *n.*, study.

Stufe, *f.*, step.

Stuhl, *m.*, chair.

Stümper, *m.*, botcher, bungler.

Stunde, *f.*, hour.

Sturm, *m.*, storm; violence, tumult.

stürmen, to attack.

Sturmvogel, *m.* (storm-bird), stormy petrel.

stürzen, to fall.

stützen, to support, rest.

Subskribent', *m.*, subscriber.

suchen, to seek, look for.

Sui-Hong, Sui-Hong (proper name).

Sünde, *f.*, sin.

Sünder, *m.*, sinner.

Sündflut, *f.*, deluge.

sündhaft, sinful.

süß, sweet.

T.

Ta'fel, *f.*, table, board.
Tag, *m.*, day.
täg'lich, daily.
Talent', *n.*, talent, genius.
Tambourin' *n.* tambourine.
Tan'ne, *f.*, pine.
Tan'nenholz, *n.*, pine-wood.
Tan'nenwald, *m.*, pine-forest.
Tan'te, *f.*, aunt.
Tanz, *m.*, dance.
tan'zen, to dance.
Tas'so, Tasso (poet).
Tau'be, *f.*, dove.
tau'send, thousand.
Teil, *m.*, part.
Tem'pel, *m.*, temple.
Tep'pich, *m.*, carpet, tapestry.
Teu'fel, *m.* (devil), fellow.
Thal, *n.*, valley.
Tha'ler, *m.*, dollar.
Thea'ter, *n.*, theatre.
Them'se, *f.*, Thames (river).
Thor, Thor (Northern deity).
Thor, *n.*, gate, city-gate.
Thrä'ne, *f.*, tear.
Thron, *m.*, throne.
Thron'saal, *m.*, throne-hall.
thu'en (that — gethan), to do.
Thü'r(e *f.*, door.
ticktack ticktack!
tief, deep.
Tie'fe, *f.*, depth.
Tier, *n.*, animal.
Tirol', the Tyrol (country).
Toch'ter, *f.*, daughter.

Tob, *m.*, death.
To'denstille, *f.*, silence of the grave.
To'des-Hym'ne, *f.*, funeral hymn, funeral dirge.
To'beskampf, *m.*, death-struggle.
töb'lich, deadly.
Ton, *m.*, sound, song.
tö'nen, to sound (forth).
Ton'künstler, *m.*, musician, composer of music.
Ton'ne, *f.*, cask, keg.
tot, dead.
To'te, *m.* and *f.*, dead person; dead man, dead woman.
tö'ten, to kill.
tö'tend, deadly.
To'tengräber, *m.*, grave-digger.
tra'gen (trug — getragen), to carry, bear, wear.
Tra'giter, *m.*, tragedian.
tra'gisch, tragic.
Tragö'die, *f.*, tragedy
Trag'sessel, *m.*, sedan-chair.
trän'ken, to give to drink, to water.
Trau'er, *f.*, grief, sorrow.
Trau'erfahne, *f.*, mourning flag.
Trau'erflor *m.*, mourning crape.
Trau'erguirlande, *f.*, mourning garland.
Trau'erweide, *f.*, weeping-willow.
trau'lich, comfortable, cosy.
träu'men, to dream.
trau'rig, sad.
trei'ben (trieb — getrieben), to drive, float, drift, carry on; sein Spiel treiben, to play.
tren'nen, to separate.

Trep'pe, *f.*, stairs, stair-case.
tre'ten (trat — getreten), to step, come.
trip'peln, to trip.
Tro'ckenheit, *f.*, dryness.
Trom'mel, *f.*, drum.
tropf! drip!
trop'fen, to drip.
Trophä'e, *f.*, trophy.
Trost, *m.*, comfort, consolation.
Trup'pe, *f.*, troop, band.
Trut'hahn, *m.*, turkey.
Tuilerie'en (*plu.*), Tuileries.
(fich) **tum'meln**, to tumble, gambol.
Tür'ke, *m.*, Turk.
Turm, *m.*, tower.

U.

ü'ber, over; across.
überall', everywhere.
überbli'cken, to look over, survey.
Ü'berfahrt, *f.*, passage.
Ü'bergang, *m.*, transition; shade, tint.
Ü'berrock, *m.*, overcoat.
überschrei'ten (überschritt — überschritten), to exceed.
Überse'tzung, *f.*, translation.
übertäu'ben, to drown (by noise).
übertref'fen (übertraf — übertroffen), to excel.
überzeu'gen, to convince; davon überzeugen, to convince of it.
überzie'hen (überzog — überzogen), to cover.
Ü'berzug, *m.*, cover, bed-cover.

ü'brig, left; übrig bleiben, to be left.
U'fer, *n.*, bank, shore.
Uhr, *f.*, clock, watch.
um, about, around; for; in order to, to; um und um, over and over, upside down.
Umar'mung, *f.*, embrace.
umflat'tern, to flutter around.
umge'ben (umgab — umgeben), to surround, enclose.
um'gekehrt, upturned; upside down.
umher', around.
umher'*blicken, to look around.
Um'riß, *m.*, sketch, outline; flüchtige Umrisse, mere outlines.
(fich) **um'*schauen**, to look around.
umschlie'ßen (umschloß — umschlossen), to enclose, surround.
umschlin'gen (umschlang — umschlungen), to enclose, surround.
un'beweglich, motionless.
un'billig, unfair.
und, and.
un'fruchtbar, uneatable, unfit for enjoyment, useless, good for nothing.
un'geheuer, immense, prodigious, huge.
un'gesäuert, unleavened.
un'gezogen, naughty, ill-mannered.
un'glücklich, unhappy, unfortunate, poor, bad.
Un'hold, *m.*, monster; goblin.
Uniform', *f.*, uniform.
Un'kraut, *n.*, weed.
uns, us; (to, for, with) us.
un'schön, unfair, vulgar.

Un′ſchuld, *f.,* innocence.
un′ſer, unſere, unſer, our.
Unſterb′lichfeit, *f.,* immortality.
un′ten, below.
un′ter, under; among.
unterbre′chen (unterbrach — unter-
brochen), to interrupt.
un′tergeordnet, inferior, subordi-
nate.
Un′terſchrift, *f.,* subscription. inscription.
un′veränderlich, unchangeable, un-
alterable.
un′verändert, unchanged.
un′vergleichlich, incomparable.
un′verfennbar, unmistakable,
evident.
un′vernünftig, unreasonable,
absurd.
un′wirtlich, (inhospitable), dreary.
üp′pig, luxuriant, exuberant.
Up′ſala, Upsal, Upsala (city).
Ur′teil, *n.,* judgment. — „Gericht
und Urteil, court and judgment,"
a play.
u. ſ. w. (und ſo weiter), and so on,
and so forth.

B.

Ba′ſe, *f.,* vase.
Ba′ter, *m.,* father.
Ba′ter=un′ſer, *n.,* " Our father; " the
Lord's prayer.
Batifan′, *m.,* Vatican.
Bene′dig, Venice (city).
Be′nus, *f.,* Venus.

vera′chten, to despise.
(ſich) verbin′den (verband — verbunden), to unite.
verbrei′ten, to spread.
verdammt′, accursed, confounded.
verder′benbringend, disastrous.
Berfaſ′ſer, *m.,* author.
vergau′gen, past, last.
vergäug′lich, transient, perishable.
verge′hen (verging — vergangen),
to pass.
vergeſ′ſen (vergaß — vergeſſen), to
forget.
Bergnü′gen, *m.,* pleasure, enjoyment.
vergol′den, to gild.
Bergol′bung, *f.,* gilding.
verhül′len, to veil, cover, wrap up.
(ſich) verir′ren, to go astray, lose
one's way, be lost.
verfau′fen, to sell.
verflä′ren, to glorify.
verfüm′mert, stunted.
verfün′den, to announce, foretell.
verlan′gen, to require.
verlaſ′ſen (verließ — verlaſſen), to
leave, give up; ſich verlaſſen, to
depend on.
verle′gen, perplexed, embarrassed.
vermeh′ren, to increase.
vermiſ′ſen, to miss.
vermö′gen (vermochte — vermocht),
to be able, can.
vernich′ten, to destroy, annihilate.
verö′det, deserted.
verra′ten (verriet — verraten), to
betray.

verrückt', crazy, insane.

Vers, *m.*, verse.

(sich) verfam'meln, to assemble.

Verfamm'lung, *f.*, assembly, gathering.

verschlie'ßen (verschloß — verschlossen), to lock, shut up.

verschwin'den (verschwand — verschwunden), to vanish, disappear.

verse'hen (versah — versehen), to provide (with).

verse'tzen, to remove, transpose.

versin'ken (versank — versunken), to sink, go down; be lost, be absorbed.

verspre'chen (versprach — versprochen), to promise.

Verspre'chen, *n.*, promise.

verste'cken, to hide, conceal.

Verste'cken, *n.*, "hide-and-seek," a play.

verste'hen (verstand — verstanden), to understand.

verstimmt' ill-humored.

verstoh'len, stealthy.

Verstor'bene, *m. and f.*, dead person, departed.

verstrei'chen (verstrich — verstrichen), to pass.

Versuch', *m.*, attempt.

vertra'gen (vertrug — vertragen), to stand, endure.

(sich) verun'einigen, to quarrel, fall out.

verwan'deln, to change.

verwandt', related, kindred.

Verwandt'schaft, *f.*, relationship; family.

verwe'hen, to blow, over, cover (with snow).

verwei'len, to stay, tarry.

verwel'ken, to wither, fade away.

verwun'den, to wound.

Verzei'hung, *f.*, pardon.

verzer'ren, to distort.

Verzweif'lung, *f.*, despair.

Vesuv', *m.*, Mount-Vesuvius.

viel, much; **viele**, many.

vielleicht', perhaps.

vier, four.

Vier'eck, *n.*, square.

vier'jährig, four years old.

viert, fourth.

Vier'tel, *n.*, quarter.

vier'zehn, fourteen.

vier'zehnt, fourteenth.

Vil'la, *f.*, villa, country-seat.

Volk, *n.*, people, populace.

voll, full.

vol'lends, wholly, entirely.

vom = von dem, of the, from the, by the.

von, of, from, by; **von — aus**, from.

vor, before, in front of; ago.

vorbei', past.

vorbei'*fahren (fuhr — gefahren), to drive past, pass by.

vorbei'*jagen, to hurry by, chase past.

Vor'bote, *m.*, herald, harbinger.

vor'*enthalten (enthielt — enthalten), to withhold.

(fich) vor'*finden (fand — gefunden), to be found.

vor'*gehen (ging — gegangen), to go on, take place.

vorhan'den, existing, actual, obvious.

Vor'hang, m., curtain; bed-curtain..

vo'rig, last, preceding.

vor'*kommen (kam — gekommen), to seem, appear.

vor'nehm, distinguished.

Vor'schein, m., appearance; zum Vorschein kommen, to appear.

Vor'stadt, f., suburbs.

vor'*stellen, to represent.

Vor'stellung, f., play, show.

vortreff'lich, excellent, splendid.

vorü'ber*fahren (fuhr — gefahren), to drive past.

vorü'ber*schreiten (schritt — geschritten), to walk by, go past.

vorü'ber*springen (sprang — gesprungen), to hurry by.

vorü'ber*ziehen (zog — gezogen), to pass by.

vor'wärts, forward.

vor'*ziehen (zog — gezogen), to prefer, like better.

vorzüg'lich, excellent.

Bre'ta, Vreta (conventual church).

W.

Wa'che, f., watch, guard.

wach'sen (wuchs — gewachsen), to grow.

Wachs'terze, f., wax-taper, candle.

wa'gen, to dare, risk.

Wa'gen, m., wagon; car; carriage.

Wa'genrad, n., carriage-wheel.

Wa'genschuppen, m., repository.

wäh'len, to choose, elect.

wahr, true.

wäh'ren, to last.

wäh'rend, during; while.

Wahr'heit, f., truth.

wahr'scheinlich, probable.

Wald, m., woods, forest.

Wal'fisch, m., whale

Wal'roß, n., walrus, sea-horse.

wäl'zen, to roll.

Wand, f., wall.

wan'dern, to wander.

Wand'uhr, f., wall-clock.

Wan'ge, f., cheek.

warm, warm.

was? what? what.

Wä'sche, f., wash; linen.

Was'ser, n., water.

Was'serfläche, f., surface of the water.

Was'serflasche, f., water-bottle.

Was'serstrahl, m., jet of water.

wech'seln, to alternate, change.

Weg, m., way.

weg, away.

we'gen, on account of.

weg'*stechen (stach — gestochen), to cut away; remove by cutting.

weg'*tanzen = hinweg'*tanzen, to dance over (the grave), perform a funeral dance.

we'hen, to blow.

Weh'mut, f., sadness.

weh'mütig, sad, sorrowful.

Weib, *n.*, woman, wife.

Wei'de, *f.*, willow.

Wei'denbaum, *m.*, willow-tree.

Wei'dengestrüpp, *n.*, thicket of willow-trees.

Wei'hekuß, *m.*, kiss of devotion; der Liebe Weihekuß, kiss of devoted love.

wei'hen, to consecrate.

Weih'wasser, *n.*, holy water.

wei'len, to stay, tarry.

wei'nen, to weep.

Wein'raufe, *f.*, vine-branch.

weiß (ich), I know; er weiß, he knows.

weiß (*adj.*), white.

weit, far, long, much; weit schöner, much more beautiful.

wei'ter, further, longer, more.

wel'cher, –e, –es, who; which.

welk, withered, dead.

Wel'le, *f.*, wave, billow.

Welt, *f.*, world.

Welt'leben, *n.*, life of man.

Welt'meer, *n.*, ocean.

wen, whom, which.

wen'den (wandte — gewandt), to turn; sich wenden, to turn one's self, address.

we'nig, little; wenige, a few, several.

wenn, when; if.

wer, who.

wer'den (ward [wurde] — geworden), to become; shall; be.

wer'fen (warf — geworfen), to throw, cast.

Werk, *n.*, work.

We'sen, *n.*, being, creature.

wi'ckeln, to wrap.

wie, how, as, like.

wie'der, again.

wie'der*geben (gab — gegeben), to render, express.

wie'der*hallen, to echo, re-echo, resound.

wiederho'len, to repeat, reiterate.

Wie'ge, *f.*, cradle.

wild, wild, spirited.

Wild, *n.*, wild animals, game.

willkom'men, welcome.

Wind, *m.*, wind.

Wind'stille, *f.*, calm.

Win'kel, *m.*, corner.

Win'ter, *m.*, winter.

wir, we.

wir'beln, to whirl.

Wir'ken, *n.*, work, working, activity.

wirk'lich, real, genuine.

Wirk'lichkeit, *f.*, reality.

wi'schen to wipe.

wis'sen (*pres.*, ich weiß; *impf.*, wußte; *p. p.*, gewußt), to know.

Wit'wenschleier, *m.*, widow's veil.

Wit'wer, *m.*, widower.

wo? where? where.

wo'chenlang, for weeks.

Wo'ge, *f.*, wave, billow.

wo'gen, to wave.

woher'? from where? whence?

wohin'? whither?

wohl, well, indeed, perhaps, (I wonder).

wohl'gebaut, well-formed, well-shaped.

woh'nen, to live; die Wohnenden, those living.

Woh'nung, _f._, dwelling, residence.

wöl'ben, to arch, bend.

Wol'fe, _f._, cloud.

wol'len (_pres._, ich will; _impf._, wollte; _p. p._, gewollt), to be willing, will, wish.

wonach', after (at, about, regarding) which _or_ what.

worau', where (up)on, whereby; by, on, of, to, against which _or_ what.

worauf', whereupon, upon which _or_ what.

wor'ben = geworden, _p. p._, been, become.

worin', wherein; in which _or_ what.

Wort, _n._, word.

wu'chern, to grow exuberantly.

Wun'de, _f._, wound.

wün'schen, to wish, desire.

wür'digen, to favor, honor, deem worthy.

wür'feln, to play at dice; to dice.

Wurm, _m._, worm.

wurm'stichig, worm-eaten, rotten.

Wü'ste, _f._, desert.

3.

Zahl, _f._, number.

zahl'reich, numerous.

zahm, tame.

zart, tender, delicate, soft, fine.

Zau'berschnecke, _f._, magic snail.

zehn, ten.

zehnt, tenth.

Zei'chen, _n._, sign, signal, landmark.

zeich'nen, to draw, sketch, design.

zei'gen, to show, point out; sich zeigen, to appear.

Zei'le, _f._, line.

Zeit, _f._, time.

Zeit'alter, _n._, age, period, era.

Zei'tung, _f._, newspaper.

Zei'tungsblatt, _n._, newspaper.

Zelt, _n._, tent.

zerbre'chen (zerbrach — zerbrochen), to break (to pieces).

zerna'gen, to gnaw to pieces, honeycomb.

zerrei'ßen (zerriß — zerrissen), to tear to pieces.

zersprin'gen (zersprang — zersprungen), to break to pieces.

zerstie'ben (zerstob — zerstoben), to be scattered (as dust or spray).

zertrüm'mern, to destroy (by gnawing).

Zeu'ge, _m._, witness; Zeuge sein, to witness, be present.

zie'hen (zog — gezogen), to pull, draw; move, float.

Zim'mer, _n._, room.

Zinn, _n._, tin.

zi'scheln, to whisper.

zot'tig, shaggy, shaggy-haired.

zu, to, at, too; zum = zu dem; zur = zu der.

zu'cken, to move convulsively, quiver, writhe.

zuer'st, at first.

Zug, *m.*, train; = Gesichtszug, feature.

Zügel, *m.*, rein.

zugegen, present.

zuletzt', at last, finally.

zu'*machen, to close, shut.

Zunge, *f.*, tongue.

zu'*nicken, to nod to, express *or* impart by nodding.

zürnen, to be angry with.

zurück'*biegen (bog — gebogen), to bend back; sich zurückbiegen, to bend back.

zurück'*kehren, to come back, return.

zurück'*schieben (schob — geschoben), to push back.

(sich) zurück'*ziehen (zog — gezogen), to withdraw.

zusam'men, together; to the ground

zusam'men*fügen, to join together.

zusam'men*sinken (sank — gesunken), to fall to the ground.

zu'*sehen (sah — gesehen), to look on, watch.

zu'*stellen, to hand to, deliver up to.

zu'*werfen (warf — geworfen), to throw to.

zu'*ziehen (zog — gezogen), to draw to, draw *or* pull tight.

zwan'zigst, twentieth.

zwar, indeed, of course, though.

zwei, two.

Zweig, *m.*, twig, branch.

zweit, second.

zwi'schen, between.

zwit'schern, to twitter.

zwölft, twelfth.

Heath's Modern Language Series.

Introduction prices are quoted unless otherwise stated.

GERMAN GRAMMARS AND READERS.

Joynes-Meissner German Grammar. A *working* Grammar, sufficiently elementary for the beginner, and sufficiently complete for the advanced student. Half leather. $1.12.

Alternative Exercises. Can be used, for the sake of change, instead of those in the *Joynes-Meissner* itself. 54 pages. 15 cts.

Joynes's Shorter German Grammar. Part I of the above. Half leather. 80 cts.

Harris's German Lessons. Elementary Grammar and Exercises for a short course, or as introductory to advanced grammar. Cloth. 60 cts.

Sheldon's Short German Grammar. For those who want to begin reading as soon as possible and have had training in some other languages. Cloth. 60 cts.

Babbitt's German at Sight. A syllabus of elementary grammar, with suggestions and practice work for reading at sight. Paper. 10 cts.

Faulhaber's One Year Course in German. A brief synopsis of elementary grammar, with exercises for translation. Cloth. 60 cts.

Meissner's German Conversation. Not a *phrase* book nor a *method* book, but a scheme of rational conversation. Cloth. 75 cts.

Harris's German Composition. Elementary, progressive, and varied selections, with full notes and vocabulary. Cloth. 50 cts.

Hatfield's Materials for German Composition. Based on *Immensee* and on *Höher als die Kirche.* Paper. 33 pages. Each 12 cts.

Stüven's Praktische Anfangsgründe. A conversational beginning book with vocabulary and grammatical appendix. Cloth. 203 pages. 70 cts.

Guerber's Märchen und Erzählungen, I. With vocabulary and questions in German on the text. Especially adapted to young beginners. Cloth. 162 pages. 60 cts.

Guerber's Märchen und Erzählungen, II. With vocabulary. Follows the above or serves as independent reader. Cloth. 202 pages. 65 cts.

Joynes's German Reader. Begins very easy, is progressive both in text and notes contains complete selections in prose and verse, and has a complete vocabulary, with appendixes, also English Exercises based on the text. Half leather. 90 cts.

Deutsch's Colloquial German Reader. Anecdotes as a basis for colloquial work, followed by tables of phrases and idioms, and a select reader of prose and verse, with notes and vocabulary. Cloth. 90 cts.

Boisen's German Prose Reader. Easy, correct, and interesting selections of graded prose, with copious notes, and an Index to the notes which serves as a vocabulary. Cloth. 90 cts.

Spanhoofd's Lehrbuch der deutschen Sprache. Grammar, conversation and exercises, with vocabulary for beginners. Cloth. 000 pages. 00 cts.

Grimm's Märchen and **Schiller's Der Taucher** (Van der Smissen). Bound one volume. Notes and vocabulary. The Märchen in Roman type; Der Taucher German type. 65 cts.

Heath's German-English and English-German Dictionary. Fully for the ordinary wants of the student. Cloth. Retail price, $1.50.

Heath's Modern Language Series.

Introduction prices are quoted unless otherwise stated.

ELEMENTARY GERMAN TEXTS.

Grimm's Märchen and **Schiller's Der Taucher** (Van der Smissen). Bound in one volume. Notes and vocabulary. The Märchen in Roman type; Der Taucher in German type. 65 cts.

Andersen's Märchen (Super). Easy German, free from antiquated and dialectical expressions. With notes and vocabulary. Cloth. 70 cts.

Andersen's Bilderbuch ohne Bilder. With notes and vocabulary by Dr. Wilhelm Bernhardt, Washington, D. C. Boards. 130 pages. 30 cts.

Leander's Träumereien. Fairy tales with notes and vocabulary by Professor Van der Smissen, of the University of Toronto. Boards. 180 pages. 40 cts.

Volkmann's Kleine Geschichten. Four very easy tales, with notes and vocabulary by Dr. Wilhelm Bernhardt, Washington, D. C. Boards. 99 pages. 30 cts.

Storm's Immensee. With notes and vocabulary by Dr. Wilhelm Bernhardt, Washington, D. C. 120 pages. Cloth, 50 cts.; boards, 30 cts.

Heyse's L'Arrabbiata. With notes and vocabulary by Dr. Wilhelm Bernhardt, Washington, D. C. Boards. 80 pages. 25 cts.

Von Hillern's Höher als die Kirche. With notes by S. W. Clary, and with a vocabulary. Boards. 106 pages. 25 cts.

Hauff's Der Zwerg Nase. With introduction by C. H. Grandgent, Director of Modern Language Instruction, Boston Public Schools. No notes. Paper. 44 pages. 15 cts.

Hauff's Das kalte Herz. With notes and vocabulary by Professor Van der Smissen of the University of Toronto. Boards. 192 pages. (In Roman type.) 40 cts.

Ali Baba and the Forty Thieves. With introduction by C. H. Grandgent, Director of Modern Language Instruction, Boston Public Schools. No notes. Paper. 53 pages. 20 cts.

Schiller's Der Taucher. With notes and vocabulary by Professor Van der Smissen of the University of Toronto. Paper. 24 pages. 12 cts.

Schiller's Der Neffe als Onkel. With notes and vocabulary by Professor H. S. Beresford-Webb of Wellington College, England. Paper. 128 pages. 30 cts.

Baumbach's Waldnovellen. Six little stories, with notes and vocabulary by Dr. Wilhelm Bernhardt. Boards. 161 pages. 35 cts.

Frommel's Eingeschneit. With notes and vocabulary, by Dr. Wilhelm Bernhardt. Boards. 000 pages. *In press.*

Spyri's Rosenresli. With notes and vocabulary for beginners, by Helene H. Boll, of the High School, New Haven, Conn. Boards. 62 pages. 25 cts.

Spyri's Moni der Geissbub. With vocabulary by H. A. Guerber. Boards. 76 pages. 25 cts.

Zschokke's Der zerbrochene Krug. With notes, vocabulary and English exercises by Professor E. S. Joynes. Boards. 88 pages. 25 cts.

Baumbach's Nicotiana *und andere Erzählungen.* Five easy stories with notes and vocabulary by Dr. Wilhelm Bernhardt. Boards. 115 pages. 30 cts.

Complete Catalogue of Modern Language texts sent on request.

Heath's Modern Language Series.

Introduction prices are quoted unless otherwise stated.

INTERMEDIATE GERMAN TEXTS.

(Partial List.)

Stille Wasser. Three tales by Krane, Hoffmann and Wildenbruch, with notes and vocabulary by Dr. Wilhelm Bernhardt. Boards. 000 pages. 00 cts.

Auf der Sonnenseite. Six humorous stories by Seidel, Sudermann, and others, with notes and vocabulary, by Dr. Wilhelm Bernhardt. Boards. 153 pages. 35 cts.

Gerstäcker's Germelshausen. With notes by Professor Osthaus, Indiana University, and with vocabulary. Boards. 83 pages. 25 cts.

Baumbach's Die Nonna. With notes and vocabulary by Dr. Wilhelm Bernhardt, Washington, D. C. Boards. 108 pages. 30 cts.

Riehl's Culturgeschichtliche Novellen. See two following texts.

Riehl's Der Fluch der Schönheit. With notes by Professor Thomas, Columbia University. Boards. 84 pages. 25 cts.

Riehl's Das Spielmannskind ; Der stumme Ratsherr. Two artistic and entertaining tales, with notes by A. F. Eaton, Oberlin College. Boards. 93 pages, 25 cts.

François's Phosphorus Hollunder. With notes by Oscar Faulhaber. Paper. 77 pages. 20 cts.

Onkel und Nichte. An original story by Oscar Faulhaber. No notes. Paper. 64 pages. 20 cts.

Ebner-Eschenbach's Die Freiherren von Gemperlein and *Krambambuli*. With introduction and notes by Professor A. R. Hohlfeld, Vanderbilt University. Boards. 138 pages. 30 cts.

Freytag's Die Journalisten. With commentary by Professor Toy of the University of North Carolina. 168 pages. Boards. 30 cts.

Schiller's Jungfrau von Orleans. With introduction and notes by Professor Wells of the University of the South. Cloth. Illustrated. 248 pages. 60 cts.

Schiller's Maria Stuart. With introduction and notes by Professor Rhoades, University of Illinois. Cloth. Illustrated. 254 pages. 60 cts.

Schiller's Wilhelm Tell. With introduction and notes by Professor Deering of Western Reserve University. Cloth. Illustrated. 280 pages. 50 cts.

Baumbach's Der Schwiegersohn. With notes by Dr. Wilhelm Bernhardt. Boards. 130 pages. 30 cts.

Plautus und Terenz; Die Sonntagsjäger. Two comedies by Benedix, and edited by Professor B. W. Wells of the University of the South. Boards. 116 pages. 25 cts.

Moser's Köpnickerstrasse 120. A comedy with introduction and notes by Professor B. W. Wells. Boards. 169 pages. 30 cts.

Moser's Der Bibliothekar. Comedy with introduction and notes by Professor B. W. Wells. Boards. 144 pages. 30 cts.

Drei kleine Lustspiele. *Günstige Vorzeichen, Der Prozess, Einer muss heiraten.* Edited with notes by Professor B. W. Wells. Boards. 126 pages. 30 cts.

Helbig's Komödie auf der Hochschule. With introduction and notes by Prof. B. W. Wells. Boards. 145 pages. 30 cts.

Complete catalogue of Modern Language texts sent on request.

Ibeath's Modern Language Series.

Introduction prices are quoted unless otherwise stated.

INTERMEDIATE GERMAN TEXTS.

(Partial List.)

Schiller's Der Geisterseher. Part I. With notes and vocabulary by Professor Joynes of South Carolina College. Paper. 124 pages. 30 cts.

Selections for Advanced Sight Translation. Short extracts compiled by Rose Chamberlin, instructor in German at Bryn Mawr College. Paper. 48 pages. 15 cts.

Selections for Sight Translation. Fifty fifteen-line extracts compiled by Mme. G. F. Mondan, High School, Bridgeport, Conn. Paper. 48 pages. 15 cts.

Benedix's Die Hochzeitsreise. With notes by Natalie Schiefferdecker, of Abbott Academy. Boards. 68 pages. 25 cts.

Arnold's Fritz auf Ferien. With notes by A. W. Spanhoofd, Director of German in the High Schools of Washington, D. C. Boards. 59 pages. 20 cts.

Aus Herz und Welt. Two stories, with notes by Dr. Wilhelm Bernhardt. Boards. 100 pages. 25 cts.

Novelletten-Bibliothek. Vol. I. Six short and interesting modern stories. Selected and edited with full notes by Dr. Wilhelm Bernhardt, Washington, D. C. Cloth. 182 pages. 60 cts.

Novelletten-Bibliothek. Vol. II. Six stories selected and edited as above. Cloth. 152 pages. 60 cts.

Unter dem Christbaum. Five Christmas Stories by Helene Stökl, with notes by Dr. Wilhelm Bernhardt, Washington, D. C. Cloth. 171 pages. 60 cts.

Hoffman's Historische Erzählungen. Four important periods of German History, with notes by Professor Beresford-Webb of Wellington College, England. Boards. 110 pages. 25 cts.

Wildenbruch's Das edle Blut. Edited with notes by Professor F. G. G. Schmidt, University of Oregon. Boards. 58 pages. 20 cts.

Wildenbruch's Der Letzte. With notes by Professor F. G. G. Schmidt, of the University of Oregon. Boards. 78 pages. 25 cts.

Stifter's Das Haidedorf. A little prose idyl, with notes by Professor Heller of Washington University, St. Louis. Paper. 54 pages. 20 cts.

Chamisso's Peter Schlemihl. With notes by Professor Primer of the University of Texas. Boards. 100 pages. 25 cts.

Eichendorff's Aus dem Leben eines Taugenichts. With notes by Professor Osthaus of Indiana University. Boards. 183 pages. 35 cts.

Heine's Die Harzreise. With notes by Professor van Daell of the Massachusetts Institute of Technology. Boards. 102 pages. 25 cts.

Jensen's Die braune Erica. With notes by Professor Joynes of South Carolina College. Boards. 106 pages. 25 cts.

Holberg's Niels Klim. Selections edited by E. H. Babbitt of Columbia College. Paper. 64 pages. 20 cts.

Meyer's Gustav Adolfs Page. With full notes by Professor Heller of Washington University. Paper. 85 pages. 25 cts.

Complete Catalogue of Modern Language texts sent on request.

Heath's Modern Language Series.

Introduction prices are quoted unless otherwise stated.

ADVANCED GERMAN TEXTS.

Schiller's Ballads. With introduction and notes by Professor Johnson of Bowdoin College. Cloth. 182 pages. 60 cts.

Scheffel's Trompeter von Säkkingen. Abridged and edited by Professor Wenckebach of Wellesley College. Cloth. Illustrated. 197 pages. 70 cts.

Scheffel's Ekkehard. Abridged and edited by Professor Carla Wenckebach of Wellesley College. Cloth. Illustrated. 241 pages. 70 cts.

Freytag's Aus dem Staat Friedrichs des Grossen. With notes by Professor Hagar of Owens College, England. Boards. 123 pages. 25 cts.

Freytag's Aus dem Jahrhundert des grossen Krieges. With introduction and notes by Professor L. A. Rhoades, of the University of Illinois. Boards. 168 pages.

Freytag's Rittmeister von Alt-Rosen. With introduction and notes by Professor Hatfield of Northwestern University. Cloth. 213 pages. 70 cts.

Lessing's Minna von Barnhelm. With introduction and notes by Professor Primer of the University of Texas. Cloth. 216 pages. 60 cts.

Lessing's Nathan der Weise. With introduction and notes by Professor Primer of the University of Texas. Cloth. 338 pages. 90 cts.

Lessing's Emilia Galotti. With introduction and notes by Professor Winkler of the University of Michigan. Cloth. 169 pages. 60 cts.

Goethe's Sesenheim. From *Dichtung und Wahrheit.* With notes by Professor Huss of Princeton. Paper. 90 pages. 25 cts.

Goethe's Meisterwerke. The most attractive and interesting portions of Goethe's prose and poetical writings, with copious notes by Dr. Bernhardt of Washington. Cloth. 285 pages. $1.50.

Goethe's Dichtung und Wahrheit. (I–IV.) With introduction and notes by Professor C. A. Buchheim of King's College, London. Cloth. 339 pages. $1.00.

Goethe's Hermann und Dorothea. With introduction, notes, bibliography, and index by Professor Hewett of Cornell University. Cloth. 293 pages. 80 cts.

Goethe's Iphigenie. With introduction, notes and a bibliography by Professor L. A. Rhoades of the University of Illinois. Cloth. 170 pages. 70 cts.

Goethe's Torquato Tasso. With introduction and notes by Professor Thomas of Columbia University. Cloth. 245 pages. 75 cts.

Goethe's Faust. Part I. With introduction and notes by Professor Thomas of Columbia University. Cloth. 435 pages. $1.12.

Goethe's Faust. Part II. With introduction and notes by Professor Thomas of Columbia University. Cloth. 533 pages. $1.75.

Heine's Poems. Selected and edited with notes by Professor White of Cornell University. Cloth. 232 pages. 75 cts.

Walther's Meereskunde. (Scientific German.) With notes and vocabulary, by Susan A. Sterling, of the University of Wisconsin. Cloth. 190 pages. 75 cts.

Gore's German Science Reader. Introductory reader of scientific German. Notes and vocabulary, by Professor Gore of Columbian University. Cloth. 195 pages. 75 cts.

Hodges's Scientific German. Part I consists of exercises in German and English, the sentences being selected from text-books on science. Part II consists of scientific essays, followed by a German-English and English-German vocabulary. Cloth. 203 pages. 75 cts.

Wenckebach's Deutsche Literaturgeschichte. Vol. I (to 1100 A.D.) with *Musterstücke.* Boards. 212 pages. 50 cts.

Wenckebach's Meisterwerke des Mittelalters. Selections from translations modern German of the masterpieces of the Middle Ages. Cloth. 300 pages. $1.25

FRENCH GRAMMARS AND READERS.

Edgren's Compendious French Grammar. A *working* grammar for high school or college; adapted to the needs of the beginner and the advanced student. Half leather, $1.12.

Edgren's French Grammar, Part I. For those who wish to learn quickly to *read* French. 35 cts.

Supplementary Exercises to Edgren's French Grammar (Locard). French-English and English-French exercises to accompany each lesson. 12 cts.

Grandgent's Short French Grammar. Brief and easy, yet complete enough for all elementary work, and abreast of the best scholarship and practical experience of to-day. 60 cts. With LESSONS AND EXERCISES, 75 cts.

Grandgent's French Lessons and Exercises. Necessarily used with the SHORT FRENCH GRAMMAR. *First Year's Course for High Schools, No. 1 ; First Year's Course for Colleges, No. 1.* Limp cloth. Introduction price, each 15 cts.

Grandgent's French Lessons and Exercises. *First Year's Course for Grammar Schools.* Limp cloth. 59 pages. 25 cents. *Second Year's Course for Grammar Schools.* Limp cloth. 72 pages. 30 cts.

Grandgent's Materials for French Composition. Five graded pamphlets based on *La Pipe de Jean Bart, La dernière classe, Le Siège de Berlin, Peppino, L'Abbé Constantin,* respectively. Each, 12 cts.

Grandgent's French Composition. Elementary, progressive and varied selections, with full notes and vocabulary. Cloth. 150 pages. 50 cts.

Kimball's Materials for French Composition. Based on *Colomba,* for second year's work; based on *La Belle-Nivernaise* for third year's work. Each, 12 cts.

Storr's Hint on French Syntax. With exercises. Interleaved. Limp cloth. 30 cts.

Marcou's French Review Exercises. With notes and vocabulary. Limp cloth. 34 pages. 20 cts.

Houghton's French by Reading. Begins with interlinear, and gives in the course of the book the whole of elementary grammar, with reading matter, notes, and vocabulary. Half leather. $1.12.

Hotchkiss's Le Premier Livre de Français. A purely conversational introduction to French, for young pupils. Boards. Illustrated. 79 pages. 35 cts.

Fontaine's Livre de Lecture et de Conversation. Entirely in French. Combines Reading, Conversation, and Grammar. Cloth. 90 cts.

Fontaine's Lectures Courantes. Can follow the above. Contains Reading, Conversation, and English Exercises based on the text. Cloth. $1.00.

Lyon and Larpent's Primary French Translation Book. An easy beginning reader, with very full notes, vocabulary, and English exercises based on the latter part of the text. Cloth. 60 cts.

Super's Preparatory French Reader. Complete and graded selections of interesting French, with notes and vocabulary. Half leather. 70 cts.

French Fairy Tales (Joynes). With notes, vocabulary, and English exercises based on the text. Boards, 35 cts.

Davies's Elementary Scientific French Reader. For beginners and confined to Scientific French. With notes and vocabulary. Boards. 136 pages. 40 cts.

Heath's French-English and English-French Dictionary. Recommended at all the colleges as fully adequate for the ordinary wants of students. Cloth. Retail price, $1.50.

Ibeath's Modern Language Series.

ELEMENTARY FRENCH TEXTS.

Jules Verne's L'Expédition de la Jeune-Hardie. With notes, vocabulary, and appendixes by W. S. Lyon. Boards. 95 pages. 25 cts.

Gervais's Un Cas de Conscience. With notes, vocabulary, and appendixes by R. P. Horsley. Boards. 86 pages. 25 cts.

Génin's Le Petit Tailleur Bouton. With notes, vocabulary, and appendixes by W. S. Lyon. Paper. 88 pages. 25 cts.

Assollant's Une Aventure du Célèbre Pierrot. With notes, vocabulary, and appendixes by R. E. Pain. Paper. 93 pages. 25 cts.

Muller's Les Grandes Découvertes Modernes. Talks on Photography and Telegraphy. With notes, vocabulary, and appendixes by F. E. B. Wale. Paper. 88 pages. 25 cts.

Récits de Guerre et de Révolution. Selected and edited, with notes, vocabulary, and appendixes by B. Minssen. Paper. 91 pages. 25 cts.

Bruno's Les Enfants Patriotes. With notes, vocabulary, and appendixes by W. S. Lyon. Paper. 94 pages. 25 cts.

Bedollière's La Mère Michel et son Chat. With notes, vocabulary, and appendixes by W. S. Lyon. Boards. 96 pages. 25 cts.

Legouvé and Labiche's La Cigale chez les Fourmis. A comedy in one act, with notes by W. H. Witherby. Boards. 56 pages. 20 cts.

Labiche and Martin's Le Voyage de M. Perrichon. A comedy with introduction and notes by Professor B. W. Wells, of the University of the South. Boards. 108 pages. 25 cts.

Labiche and Martin's La Poudre aux Yeux. Comedy with notes by Professor B. W. Wells, University of the South. Boards. 92 pages. 25 cts.

Dumas's L'Evasion du Duc de Beaufort. With notes by D. B. Kitchen. Boards. 91 pages. 25 cts.

Assollant's Récits de la Vieille France. With notes by E. B. Wauton. Paper. 78 pages. 25 cts.

Berthet's Le Pacte de Famine. With notes by B. B. Dickinson. Boards. 94 pages. 25 cts.

Erckmann-Chatrian's L'Histoire d'un Paysan. With notes by W. S. Lyon. Paper. 94 pages. 25 cts.

France's Abeille. With notes by C. P. Lebon of the Boston English High School. Paper. 94 pages. 25 cts.

La Main Malheureuse. With complete and detailed vocabulary, by H. A. Guerber, Nyack, N. Y. Boards. 106 pages. 25 cts.

Enault's Le Chien du Capitaine. With notes and vocabulary, by C. Fontaine, Director of French in the High Schools of Washington, D. C. Boards. 142 pages. 35 cts.

Trois Contes Choisis par Daudet. (*Le Siège de Berlin, La dernière Classe, La Mule du Pape.*) With notes by Professor Sanderson of Harvard. Paper. 15 cts.

Halévy's L'Abbé Constantin. Edited with notes, by Professor Thomas Logie, of Rutgers College. Boards. 160 pages. 35 cts.

Erckmann-Chatrian's Le Conscrit de 1813. With notes and vocabulary b Professor O. B. Super, Dickinson College. Cloth. 216 pages. 65 cts. Boards. 45

Selections for Sight Translation. Fifty fifteen-line French extracts compil Miss Bruce of the High School, Newton, Mass. Paper. 38 pages. 15 cts.

Heath's Modern Language Series.

Introduction prices are quoted unless otherwise stated.

INTERMEDIATE FRENCH TEXTS.

(Partial List.)

About's Le Roi des Montagnes. Edited by Professor Thomas Logie. Boards. 238 pages. 40 cts.

Pailleron's Le Monde où l'on s'ennuie. A comedy with notes by Professor Pendleton of Bethany College, W. Va. Boards. 138 pages. 30 cts.

Souvestre's Le Mari de Mme de Solange. With notes by Professor Super of Dickinson College. Paper. 59 pages. 20 cts.

Historiettes Modernes, Vol. I. Short modern stories, selected and edited, with notes, by C. Fontaine, Director of French in the High Schools of Washington, D. C. Cloth. 162 pages. 60 cts.

Historiettes Modernes, Vol. II. Short stories as above. Cloth. 160 pages. 60 cts.

Fleurs de France. A collection of short and choice French stories of recent date, with notes by C. Fontaine, Washington, D. C. Cloth, 158 pages. 60 cts.

Sandeau's Mlle de la Seiglière. With introduction and notes by Professor Warren of Adelbert College. Boards. 158 pages. 30 cts.

Souvestre's Un Philosophe sous les Toits. With notes and vocabulary by Professor Frazer of the University of Toronto. Cloth. 283 pages. 80 cts. —— Without vocabulary. Cloth. 178 pages. 50 cts.

Souvestre's Les Confessions d'un Ouvrier. With notes by Professor Super of Dickinson College. Paper. 127 pages. 30 cts.

Augier's Le Gendre de M. Poirier. One of the masterpieces of modern Comedy. Edited by Professor B. W. Wells, of the University of the South. Boards. 118 pages, 30 cts.

Mérimée's Colomba. With notes by Professor J. A. Fontaine of Bryn Mawr College. 192 pages. Cloth, 60 cts.; boards, 35 cts.

Mérimée's Chronique du Règne de Charles IX. With notes by Professor P. Desages, Cheltenham College, England. Paper. 119 pages. 25 cts.

Sand's La Mare au Diable. With notes by Professor F. C. de Sumichrast of Harvard. Boards. 122 pages. 25 cts.

Sand's La Petite Fadette. With notes by F. Aston-Binns, Balliol College, Oxford, England. Boards. 142 pages. 30 cts.

De Vigny's Le Cachet Rouge. With notes by Professor Fortier of Tulane University. Paper. 60 pages. 20 cts.

De Vigny's La Canne de Jonc. Edited by Professor V. J. T. Spiers, with Introduction by Professor Cohn of Columbia University. Boards. 218 pages. 40 cts.

Complete Catalogue of Modern Language texts sent on request.

Reprint Publishing

FÜR MENSCHEN, DIE AUF ORIGINALE STEHEN.

Bei diesem Buch handelt es sich um einen Faksimile-Nachdruck der Originalausgabe. Unter einem Faksimile versteht man die mit einem Original in Größe und Ausführung genau übereinstimmende Nachbildung als fotografische oder gescannte Reproduktion.

Faksimile-Ausgaben eröffnen uns die Möglichkeit, in die Bibliothek der geschichtlichen, kulturellen und wissenschaftlichen Vergangenheit der Menschheit einzutreten und neu zu entdecken.

Die Bücher der Faksimile-Edition können Gebrauchsspuren, Anmerkungen, Marginalien und andere Randbemerkungen aufweisen sowie fehlerhafte Seiten, die im Originalband enthalten sind. Diese Spuren der Vergangenheit verweisen auf die historische Reise, die das Buch zurückgelegt hat.

ISBN 978-3-95940-095-4

Made in Germany